ARCHITECTURAL ANTIQUES

For Margaret and Lois

ARCHITECTURAL ANTIQUES

Alan Robertson

Photography by Douglas Unwin

Chronicle Books • San Francisco

First published in the United States 1987 by
Chronicle Books

**Library of Congress Cataloguing in Publication Data
available.**

ISBN 0-87701-500-7

10   9   8   7   6   5   4   3   2   1

Chronicle Books
San Francisco

Designed by **Elizabeth Palmer**
Typeset by **Tradespools Limited**
Printed and bound in Portugal by
Printer Portuguesa, Sintra

CONTENTS

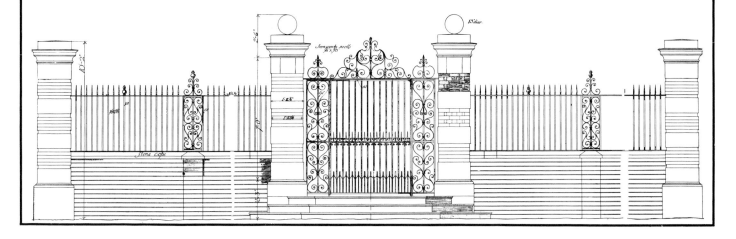

INTRODUCTION

*A converted
Methodist chapel
converted to a
comfortable family
home using re-
cycled architectural
features and
fittings. All the
bricks are
reclaimed
handmade
eighteenth-century
examples, the club
fender in front of
the central
fireplace is an altar
rail from another
church, the beams
are from an old
barn and the cast
iron panels from a
demolished country
house in Norfolk.
The windows are
new and replaced
the mediocre
quality stained
glass, so common
in mid-nineteenth
century chapels.*

Architectural antiques are relatively new in dealing and auction circles and rather defy a formal description as a group. A very simple definition is that they are fixtures and fittings in a house or garden, and as such are often attached to the house and included in the sale of the property. You may be sad to leave them behind and will probably fight to have them excluded from the sale, though, ironically, it may have been those very architectural features which attracted your buyers in the first place.

There are more grey areas in the definition of architectural antiques than the simple black and white of antique furniture. Very few specialist auction houses or dealers will keep to any rigid definition as fashions in architecture and decoration change with almost seasonal regularity and they will all try to keep up with, and even set, the trends. A brief visit to a specialist auction view or a dealer who advertises a comprehensive stock will illustrate the huge variety of bidets and bricks, windows and widgets, statues and showers that make up any collection of architectural antiques.

The dealers confuse this definition further as they are very liable to offer many other items which they have acquired on their buying forays, most of which, they hope, may yield a profit, but will have very little to do with architecture. Look at any dealer's premises and you will see how difficult it is to be precise. Even *they* do not know what will turn up tomorrow. As the majority of raw materials come from a wide range of buildings—factories, offices, government chambers, libraries, old farm cottages, pubs, restaurants, gardens of all shapes and sizes—the range of style, qualities and periods is endless. Interesting objects dating from the Middle Ages or from the Art Deco era can be found in some dusty corner.

Architectural antiques will frequently become an integral part of the fabric of a building, adding charm and character, a focal point of interest and, sometimes, antiquity. Like all antiques, they should be searched for and bought to give pleasure rather than purely collected like stamps in an album. A great deal of the pleasure is in the search itself which can be long and often comes to nothing. Along the way many other items will be found or offered and there is always the hope that the specific treasure is just around the dealer's corner. The pleasure may be in acquiring purely decorative additions to your home, rather than those with any practical use. Your friends may well think you totally mad as you scour the country looking for bricks which are 'just the right colour' or the perfect iron bracket to carry the favourite fuscia. If you do find the perfect addition, add it in a way that will allow it to be removed without too much damage and to be built again in your next house. After all the searching it can be much too nice to be lost permanently.

THE BOOM IN TRADE

T here has always been some demand for recycled architectural materials but prior to the 1970s this was generally the domain of demolition contractors who would use Victorian and Georgian doors as barricades in half-destroyed houses or turn handmade clamp bricks into hardcore or infill for a new concrete jungle. Following the lead of their American counter-parts, a few enlightened architects in England started specifying original building materials for

The interior of a dealer's yard. An enterprising customer could immediately spot some rather attractive panelling, a highly desirable corner hand basin with original brass taps, an especially fine carved wooden pelmet and a collection of pawnbrokers' signs.

restoration work which led to the establishment of co-operative materials groups in some towns and cities. Antiques dealers, seldom slack in spotting a new trend, were not slow to jump onto the bandwagon. By the mid-seventies, there were a considerable number of dealers specializing in old baths, bricks and beams and old bits and pieces rescued from demolished pubs and houses, some stately, some suburban. Many of these specialist dealers started commercial life in towns and cities with an established architectural heritage: the happy combination of supply and demand in one centre.

It became easier to buy almost anything from a house or commercial property without all the strange looks that frequently accompanied a visit to a demolition site ten years earlier. In those bad old days, if you asked a demolition worker 'how much do you want for that old iron bracket?' the response would be one of veiled disbelief and then, usually, a refusal to sell. The next moment the iron ball would smash through the wall, the desirable bracket would shatter into a million pieces and be lost for ever. The motive was, one must assume, part of the demolisher's mentality and based on the age-old attitude that if it's worth something to you it must be worth more to me! As he was unwilling to admit that he did not know the market value, better to destroy out of hand. Today the demolition worker is much less willing to simply destroy and consequently more material enters the marketplace. However, demolition is a hard-headed and highly competitive business and getting the job done on time and on budget is still more important than saving some old bits and pieces.

The best way to get the feel of the business and to get an inkling of the vast variety of materials available is to visit three or four dealers and browse among their stocks. It is probably grossly unfair to select one dealer from among hundreds of fine businesses, but there is one in Bath in England which would appear to set a standard and, more especially, a philosophy of business which could be repeated in any large town or city. Bath is renowned worldwide for its fine Georgian crescents and architecture and, more especially, for the care and interest lavished on many of its fine buildings. The company is Walcot Reclamation, which operates from a Victorian builder's yard close to Shakespeare's River Avon. The jumbled mass of warehouses and store rooms display, if that is the

Architectural salvage comes in all manner of shapes and sizes.

An almost indescribable assemblage of architectural antiques and collectables awaiting the enterprising decorator. The list is endless but extends from church organ pipes to chimney pots and even a cast iron sign from a gentleman's public lavatory.

right word under their circumstances, a vast cornucopia of doors and dados, stained glass and staircases, panels and pediments, baths and bricks—everything which could possibly be built into a period home, with quite a few pieces defying any possible practical purpose.

What makes Walcot unique and in many ways different to other similar good dealers is the combination of trades and skills on the premises. A wide variety of self-employed specialists have been encouraged to use workshop space in the project and offer their particular skills to the restoration and repair of the hundreds of period artifacts stocked and sold there. Another part of their philosophy which could well be copied is

its willingness to stock other than period items. Among all the fine Georgian and Victorian artifacts you are quite liable to find plastic door handles from the fifties. Restorers in the future will praise their foresight!

In a practical sense, if you intend seriously visiting a dealer, remember that you are almost bound to be tempted with something and it is essential that you make up your mind to buy at that time. Always carry vital measurements of every room in the project so that the decision can be made in total confidence. If you leave the unique piece to go back and measure above the chimneypiece the next visitor is almost bound to buy it immediately.

ANTIQUE BUILDING MATERIALS

Building with antique architectural features makes a great deal of sense. Not only are the components less expensive, they are frequently of better quality, and the finished result is actually worth more money than the same house built in new materials. The timber will have matured and will be less liable to shrink or twist—there will certainly be old nails and

A mews development in Yorkshire built by a local antique dealer utilizing reclaimed materials including bricks, doors, roof tiles and chimney pots. Virtually the only new materials used were the main structural timbers, guttering and down-pipes and windows. The Regency period wrought iron panels surrounding the front of the house had been kept in stock for four years waiting to be used in just the right way.

Old farm and stable doors about to be incorporated in a barn to house conversion. The barred example is most attractive but could, perhaps, present draught-proofing problems.

antique bricks were moulded by hand, wood was hand sawn, stone and slate hewn by hand—all have gained that individual texture that goes hand-in-hand with handwork plus that wonderful bonus—the patina of wind and weather, polishing and wear, over the years. This patina and lived-in look cannot be replicated by modern reproduction materials.

WHERE TO LOOK

In general terms, the basics are best found at the dealers who specialize in bricks, stone, or timber. It may sound rather obvious but it does not often pay to buy in odd lots from amateurs or private sales. The specialists have the expertise to advise you, they have the machinery to move and pack the materials without further damage and they should have the stock from which to make a detailed selection. In many cases it is not what you buy but what you leave behind that really counts. If you find towards the end of a specific job that you are short of materials it may well be possible to go back to the dealer and buy more from the original stock. The colour will match, the design will match and you will end up with a complete construction from one original source.

The extras, the windows, the doors, staircases, and all the important bits and pieces that combine to add interest and value to the property will come from an architectural antique dealer. The same lessons apply when you come to examine his stock. You will get first-class service if you explain the project at the onset—bring your architect's plans with you and make it clear that you are 'in the market' to buy. He will have seen too many time-wasters around his, no doubt, fascinating premises over the years, and will always welcome a genuinely interested buyer. Most architectural antique dealers are not in the business purely to make money but because they love what they do. They admire the workmanship that has been captured in the fine old materials, they frequently remark that 'they don't make them like this any more', and many have a real desire to see the architectural heritage of yesterday saved and re-used. If they can make an honest penny or three along the way, good luck to them and long may they prosper. For far too long have fine old buildings been torn down to be replaced by the concrete and glass of today without a thought of saving and re-using the precious bricks and stone, glass and slate, the very soul of the old.

screws to remove—and you are almost certain to miss one and completely ruin your very best saw. All the bricks and stone will have to be cleaned which is certainly a slow, dirty and totally thankless task. You will find the slates you want after weeks of searching and you will be twenty short to complete the job! Every door and every window will vary slightly in size—not a lot—just enough to make every job take twice as long as you estimated. But after all the trauma, the finished house will be worth all the heartache, all the searching, all the bargaining with hard-hearted demolition dealers and all the other tiny disappointments you've gone through. All your

POTENTIAL

Property values confirm that houses built with recycled materials command a premium price, but even if the entire house is not built with old bricks and stone, the addition of some interesting architectural feature can improve the aesthetic appearance and the value of the property. This addition could be some 'important' gates, some garden statuary or a gazebo, or a simple and inexpensive item. An otherwise quite ordinary little cottage in Yorkshire features a school clock set into the wall near its front door. As cars pass they slow down and newcomers are shown 'the cottage with the clock in it'. This charming notoriety presumably also increases the property's potential value as well as being an interesting architectural feature.

VARIATIONS

There are obviously countless variations in old building materials and architectural antiques.

Important variations that should be considered are building out of period and building out of geographical context. Both are very much at the discretion of the owner and the planning or zoning authorities. How far can you take the use of old materials and when does their use cease to make any economic or practial sense? Is a façade of old bricks on an ultra-efficient core the answer, or do you build to a contemporary design with old recycled materials? The same arguments apply to imported materials—should you only use the local brick or stone, or would materials from further afield blend well with your surroundings? The cost of moving heavy building materials probably prohibits too much importation but there are some unique local materials—stone, slate, marble, for instance—which can prove irresistible to a visiting would-be builder and can certainly add interest and excitement to any new home.

RESTORATION

Assuming that the building materials have been cleaned and the timber de-nailed, ensure that your architect is fully conversant with old building methods and practices, although this is not to say that everything has to be used in its original form or purpose. One of the great joys is breaking the rules and finding a new use for old materials.

Look for architectural objects and features long before you actually need them! It makes real sense to collect and stockpile all sorts of bits and pieces, statues and tiles, brackets and friezes before you build. It is very much easier to build the space than it is to find the right-sized object to fill it! One of the most dramatic early examples of the extensive use of recycled architectural antiques took place in the mid-seventies in a small town in Yorkshire. A Hollywood attorney bought a complete street of period houses, and then demolished every second building to create open space before he created a Port Merion-Style townscape using a collection of bizarre objects collected from all over Europe. Before building actually started, the entire collection had been amassed and filled two disused cinemas. When construction started, it was possible to build a wall and doorway to fit the beautiful circular Turkish door, to design and construct a niche to display the Greek statue, to design a porchway around the collection of ironwork panels, and so on. The moral is collect today, build tomorrow.

The vast majority of homes feature relatively plain roofs—enlivened only, in some cases, by decorative crestings and chimney stacks. Here, however, the decorative themes of the window surrounds and house architecture have been mirrored in the interesting tile designs and patterns on the roof.

13

THE HISTORY OF A PIECE

A selection of gilded overmantle mirrors are always a popular feature at Brillscote Farm Auctions in Wiltshire. The central mirror reflects a stripped pine Georgian rocking horse. To the right is a pine water-urn stand from Provence containing four terracotta ewers.

ABOVE LEFT AND LEFT. The gigantic bronze and iron bust of Napoleon's General Francois Marie Casimir Negrier. It was originally erected in the main square of Le Mans in 1857 until it was removed by German troops during the Second World War to use the bronze for their war effort. Finding that the bronze was only a thin skin over cast iron, they abandoned it, and it was only discovered in a French farmhouse in 1986.

15

A pulpit in a village church in Wales (LEFT) was imaginatively transformed to become an integral part of a San Francisco pizza parlour (RIGHT).

16

The huge wrought iron hinges from the west door of St. Wilfrid's Church in York (ABOVE) find a new home on the garage doors of the author's home. The iron gate is from the baptistery of the same church. The original narrow gates had to be joined together to form one 'normal' size gate—the overthrow will have to find a new role as a wellhead in the garden.

BRICKWORK

Bricks are probably the most popular and successful building material in architectural history although they are constantly in and out of fashion. Currently, they are very much in vogue. Available in the widest possible range of colours, textures, sizes and shapes, they are used to add a special mellow character to any building.

WHERE TO LOOK

Most demolition contractors, specialist building material dealers and most architectural antique suppliers will have stocks of cleaned, usually local, period bricks, ranging from handmade Tudor period ones to modern machine-made examples.

This is one of the areas of architecture where the modern replica is possibly less expensive, less trouble and certainly more efficient to use than the original product. New bricks are often almost indistinguishable from original ones and come in diverse shapes for rounded columns and twisted chimney stacks as well as ornamental plaques, decorated patterned surfaces and so forth.

If you consider using replica bricks in a major reconstruction or a new building, try and see them actually in use as it is hard to get a true impression of their appearance from the new samples in the suppliers' showrooms. A good supplier should be able to indicate a development where they have been used recently and, assuming that a competent builder was involved, some impression of the finished look can be seen. It is equally important to see the quality of the builder's or bricklayer's work. The very best and most expensive bricks in the market will not survive the ministrations of a less than sympathetic builder. Mistakes made at this stage are very expensive to rectify and disheartening to boot.

POTENTIAL

Bricks can be used successfully both inside or out; they have the advantage of easy construction, long life and little or no maintenance for a relatively long time. Charming and unique features can be built in almost any situation by a clever architect using special bricks, made to order in a multitude of shapes, textures and colours. The best thing is to look around at styles, see what you like, take a photograph and show it to your architect, builder or the bricklayer.

VARIATIONS

The colour and texture of period bricks depends to a great extent on the clays used, the processes used in manufacture, the heat of the kiln, and even the fuel—coal or wood or town garbage. The texture of the brick face and the colour of the mortar used determine the effect of sunlight and shadow on the structure and hence the colour effect. The mortar will need to be raked out in some old walls and replaced using the same colour and composition. This assists in ridding the wall of unwanted moisture which will prove damaging in the long term.

Beware of uncleaned bricks still thick with old mortar. While it is relatively easy to remove compared to modern mixes, it is still a costly and painstaking task. It is best to buy cleaned and sorted bricks and to avoid paint-marked or damaged bricks which have not been treated with respect. Even old bricks can suffer from white salt deposits seeping out. A change of prevailing wind or location can often bring out dormant mineral salts even in established old bricks.

RESTORATION

The restoration of individual bricks is almost never worthwhile except, perhaps, with rare, shaped examples in very small quantities when a special order is not cost-effective. It is far easier to choose suitable reproductions or replicas

Reclaimed handmade bricks are used here with great effect to bring warmth and interest to this English country cottage, built entirely from old rescued materials. The Victorian cast iron fireplace was restored and built in together with its surrounding ceramic tiles. The bricks have been used to form interesting arched windows, emphasized by the festoon blinds in Laura Ashley fabric.

19

made to the same design. Remember that these can be coloured with water or alcohol-based dyes, but always try this first on one or two bricks, and not on bricks *in situ*. Bricks exposed inside a building can be sealed to prevent dusting of the brick itself and, more especially, the mortar. Investigate the different methods of pointing as nothing can make or mar brickwork more than the pointing. Cutting back the pointing delineates the shape and texture of the brick and can look most attractive. Exterior pointing can change the surface colour of the brick by altering the water penetration, and inside it is probably best used on exposed feature walls.

Look for good match of colour, size and textures, and above all employ a good bricklayer who understands and can point period bricks.

ABOVE. A highly unusual use for old roof slates: laid on end and embedded in concrete they create interest and shadows under an arbor in an English garden.
LEFT. More than almost any other building material, bricks add the warmth so traditional in English architecture. No more so than in the welcome they suggest as you arrive at a fine hotel—in this case, Middlethorpe Hall.

LEFT. Brickwork from a variety of periods. From the top: Roman bricks mixed with flints; regular Roman bricks; fifteenth-century brickwork; eighteenth-century chequer brickwork. BELOW. A fine example of English brickwork in an award-winning hotel restoration.

STONEWORK

Stonework can be used as an architectural antique in two ways: as a facing or building material for both interior and exterior use, or as a carved architectural ornamental feature.

WHERE TO LOOK
All the usual architectural antique trade sources will have a full selection of carvings, niches, and finials, removed from a variety of buildings,

Four stone griffons removed from the front of a bank building in Leeds which are cut to form the supporting base of a circular stone trough. Over the years lichens and mosses have covered and welded the joints. To the rear is an interesting stone garden seat made from a badly broken stone trough.

OPPOSITE. A group of nineteenth-century garden ornaments in a specialist architectural auction of Sotheby's. In the foreground is one of a pair of stone lions; to the right is an exceptional pair of Albani stoneware urns decorated with bearded masks; beyond the lion are a pair of white marble classical busts of maidens; and to the left of the group is an outstanding white marble figure of Ruth by Aristide Fontana.

especially Victorian buildings and churches and chapels of all periods. If you attempt to buy directly from source, one possible avenue is the stoneyard at any old cathedral. Most major old cathedrals employ a full-time staff to maintain the fabric in good order and to look after continual restoration. This restoration frequently involves the removal of worn old finials, gargoyles and carvings, which are sometimes available for sale from the cathedral maintenance department. Monumental stonemasons are also worth checking for uncollected orders and repairs for which they might be glad to find a new home.

POTENTIAL

The very nature of stonework tends to prohibit radical change of shape in a recycled guise—the trick with ornamental stonework is to find a new and sympathetic use.

RESTORATION

Restoration, in the main, does not present any really difficult problems although it has, naturally, to be entrusted to a professional stonemason and not attempted by a layman. Exotic stonework such as alabaster, lapis lazuli, marble, jasper, and the like presents quite special cleaning and restoration requirements which will demand research and expert care.

Look for fresh marks on old stone which can easily disfigure the piece. For internal stonework choose a clean face or avoid such pieces. For outdoor pieces such marks can be aged quickly by a liberal and regular application of liquid plant food which helps in encouraging rapid moss growth.

VARIATIONS

Using stonework indoors, which has perhaps spent several hundred years atop a church spire, can present problems with continuing decay and consequent 'dusting'. The surface can be painted with a commercial floor or cement sealer to prevent this, or be brushed with a solution of sodium silicate which will have the same effect. Problems can also be caused by mosses and lichens which are desirable when stonework is used or left outdoors but will die in the dry atmosphere of a home. Lichens and mosses can be easily removed by brushing on a strong solution of ammonia but this may leave bare and rather unpleasant marks and could spoil the patination.

Beware of using any old stonework in a load-bearing structural capacity if you are in any doubt as to its strength. If any cracks are apparent, do have it checked first by an architect or structural engineer. If a crack appears in existing stonework this can be due to several factors such as the movement of the foundations or pressures from above. If the crack is wider at the bottom, it is foundation movement; if at the top, the problem rests there. In either case a *tell tale*—a strip of thin glass cemented over the crack—will break as soon as any movement occurs and it is time to call in the experts.

A pair of old gate posts with interesting and attractive detail work which could be duplicated by assiduous searching through architectural dealers' stocks.

SLATES & FLAGSTONES

WHERE TO LOOK

There are several specialist dealers in old paving and a selection of slates and flagstones can be found in most architectural antiques yards. Many local authorities maintain stocks of old paving stones and slabs and can be persuaded to part with some for a worthwhile restoration project.

Beware of thin slabs which are discoloured over half of one side. These are not paving slabs in the true sense of the word but are stone roof tiles. In England they are found mostly in the West Riding of Yorkshire but are not generally load-bearing and are not really suitable for paths and patios. They are (perhaps) attractive because of this odd discolouration and can be used, for example, on raised garden beds, and other situations which are not subject to heavy wear or weight.

Try not to buy stone slabs by weight—a popular practice with some recycling or architectural antiques dealers. Some stone flags can be extremely thick—four or more inches thick—and you may find that your investment covers a much smaller area than you anticipated.

Avoid stone disfigured by any old paintwork—this can be rather difficult to remove especially with the more porous varieties.

RESTORATION

Restoration is best left to a skilled stonemason and should not be attempted by a layman. If you are fortunate enough to buy stone flags or pavings from an original untouched source, supervise every movement and moment of their removal. Each piece should be lifted by hand and with wooden tools to prevent scratching, before being wrapped in old blankets and laid on a thick bed of straw to absorb vibration in transit. Do not pile too many on top of each other as the combined weight and a sudden bump can undo all your care and trouble.

Old Yorkshire flagstones used to effect in a garden setting combined with a collection of stone troughs and antique copper containers. Bordering on the first step down into the trough garden are two stone bosses from the roof of a local church, now demolished.

POTENTIAL

When flagstones are used inside in a kitchen or hallway, their appearance can be improved dramatically by sealing or waxing. Sealing with commercial products is probably easier than the more traditional beeswax but can present problems in areas which are not regularly used. In these parts, the sealer tends to build up with dust and dirt and you can find yourself with a clean path surrounded by rather dirty borders.

Variations can be achieved by using various laying patterns or mixing stone slabs or flags with other materials, for example bricks, gravel, or weathered wood.

Just as with a choice of antique furniture, look for colour, texture and, if possible, attractive deep patination without any recent disfiguring scratches.

The play of light and shadow is one of the most attractive features of old York stone flags used in a patio or garden setting. Although they can be used in virtually any area, frequent side lighting can provide this added dramatic bonus.

PLASTERWORK & MOULDING

WHERE TO LOOK
Many of the specialist dealers offer extensive illustrated catalogues, which usually only represent a tiny selection of their stock or examples from their store of carvings and original moulds. In many cases, they will be able to reproduce, taking a cast from your existing pattern and replicating this in the required length and design.

RESTORATION
Any restoration of period plasterwork must be carried out by a specialist and should not be undertaken by the layman. However, all the basic elements of period plasterwork, except the centuries of skill and experience, are generally available 'off the shelf' so the skilled amateur could 'restore' by replacing such items as ceiling centres, decorative trusses and the like, which can be bought complete and applied as total entities. In this way an amateur can replace part of a run of plaster cornices, for example, without the repair being visible. If you are fortunate enough to own a property with a building or decoration history, the plasterwork firm responsible for the original work may still be in existence and have the same moulding available.

POTENTIAL
There is a wealth of decorative plasterwork available from a wide selection of specialists, and many of the examples in their catalogues still cast today from the original eighteenth-century moulds. Composition ornaments, plaques and swags can be used in their natural state, painted, or even used as three-dimensional trompe l'oeil. Plaster swags can be painted to resemble limewood or pine and could achieve the effect of eighteenth-century hanging swags at a tiny fraction of the price of the originals. In practice, it is much simpler to create a large, completely

An extremely fine English plaster ceiling at Fairfax House in York dating from 1762 and restored in 1982. Especially interesting are the groups of 'champagne corks' decorating the ceiling cornice: known as gutta they are more frequently found outside in Doric capitals.

new feature—for example total room panelling, niches, columns or ornamental decorations—than it is to restore a neglected piece.

VARIATIONS

The variety of plasterwork is immense: decorated trusses, plaques representing classical or thematic subjects, urns and griffins, swags and ribbons, mythical beasts and nymphs, panel mouldings in hundreds of different designs,

architraves and dado rails, cornices, bands, columns and capitals, ceiling centres and niches.

Look for traditional mouldings and ceiling centres in polyurethane. While total anathema to the purist, they are light and easy to fit for the complete amateur and, if anything, a step in the path of true enlightenment. Unless there really is no alternative, these modern replicas should never be mixed with the genuine article.

WOODWORK

WHERE TO LOOK

The same sources apply as for basic buildings materials—the architectural antique dealers, demolition yards and material recycling groups.

Local historical societies with period houses to maintain will be happy to advise on possible suppliers. For decorative carvings, church pew ends, and smaller wooden features, try general

OPPOSITE PAGE. A corner full of architectural interest. The central carved oak corbel supports the mounted skull of a tropical barracuda; to the side hangs an Indian opium-crushing bowl in the shape of a mythical beast; the beam over the open brick fireplace is curved and possibly from the wreck of a small ship. The oil painting is of tropical birds and is on a timber panel, whilst the plant is displayed in a late eighteenth-century iron-wire jardinière.

LEFT. This warm pine panelling is made from church vestry cupboard doors. The central carving is a ship's figurehead in pine; the oval object to the right is an elephant's foot; the seated wooden figure is an early nineteenth-century artist's lay figure. A Welsh wyvern stands guard on the seventeenth-century oak kist. The ikon is Russian and the carved object on the pier below the figurehead is a small pair of Indian Rajasthan doors. The handmade bricks are modern, of Dutch design.

antique trade outlets—as a great many stock choice items in sixteenth- or seventeenth-century English oak or nineteenth-century European carvings, many of which were removed from larger pieces of furniture in the days when this was less saleable.

VARIATIONS

The woodwork available in the architectural antiques trade, while almost limitless in scope, falls roughly into three categories.

Basic building materials These include beams, trusses, flooring and mouldings, which all perform an important structural function, but are mainly chosen for their appearance and character rather than for their function.

'Enhancing woodwork' Items such as doors, architraves, skirtings, mouldings, panelling and columns, which 'enhance' their surroundings but are not strictly necessary to the construction of the building.

Decorative woodwork That of little or no structural purpose, for example decorative carvings, bosses, and corbels.

Woodwork chosen for looks rather than strength still has to be sound and free of termites, woodworm and other nasty creatures, and everything should be thoroughly checked before being introduced to your property. When choosing old timbers, be especially careful about pieces which have been stored in damp or badly ventilated positions: these are the two worst enemies of timber. Timber beams which have been attacked by woodworm should not be

discarded out of hand as they can be treated and will be perfectly safe in use. The action of the woodworm grubs can often leave a tracery of holes and tunnels (when the wood is cut) and this can add a charming dimension to the appearance of the timber, though this feature is an acquired taste and your enthusiasm may not be shared by others—especially prospective buyers! Some of the most attractive old beams, for instance, have been worm-eaten away by generations of creatures and are greatly sought after by old house restorers and by enthusiasts anxious to add some instant antiquity to their homes. Even when such a beam can no longer be trusted to be load-bearing it can still be incorporated in a purely decorative role or supported by steel reinforcements.

RESTORATION

The restoration and treatment of timber and woodwork falls into three categories. Many small pieces can be treated by the layman simply by following the instructions on the bottle. Larger examples inherited with the property may by necessity have to be restored or treated *in situ* by specialists. Larger examples not yet installed can be taken to specialist timber treatment companies for chemical baths or gas treatment. With antique furniture there are accepted, limited degrees of restoration allowable but these rules do not generally apply to architectural pieces, which have to perform a function when incorporated into a building.

When new wood is added to old it must be

blended in to the colour and grain of the original. To achieve this there is a wide variety of water or alcohol-based stains which can, with practice, match almost any two timbers from the same family together. This is especially important when matching skirtings to panelling. Panelling is sought-after and prized and therefore saved. Skirtings, however, are seldom rescued from a demolition as they have taken the brunt of wear throughout the years and are frequently fastened by cut nails which are almost impossible to remove.

Look for unusual pieces of woodwork which can be treated as architectural features: their beauty is strictly in the eye of the beholder, until they are incorporated and become the envy of all. Look, for instance, in barns and on farms for pieces of machinery which incorporate wood and metal. When these are polished on heavy-duty metal polishing machinery they can assume a wonderful patination and colour which quite belies their origins. Look also in old factories, workshops and cooperages (when the tools and equipment in making barrels are quite fascinating and totally unique to that trade). Timber and woodwork which has become worn in a specific way through use, and use only, assumes a character which cannot be duplicated in any other way. A staircase of worn old pine steps, for example, could be reused in a totally different way, the unique wear pattern almost impossible to achieve by any other method.

The symbol of plenty: the cornucopia carved on pine panels would enhance almost any decoration scheme and could become a focal interest point or a built-in feature.

33

FLOORS

Timber floors can make one of the most significant contributions to the appearance, feel and warmth of any room but must be treated with great respect. An old floor of good quality, colour and patination can be as charming as any piece of eighteenth-century furniture but it is quite another matter lifting this floor and re-establishing it in your home. Re-establishing is very much the word as more care and sympathy is required in the installation of old flooring than in its original creation. To achieve the best effect, each plank must be marked and numbered and relaid in exactly the same position—not just side by side, but in the identical position so that wear and marks, colour and fading match perfectly. As the two rooms will, no doubt, vary in size, shape and complexity, the difficulty involved will be immediately apparent.

It is, of course, quite possible to buy a section of old flooring and relay this as one would use new timber. The result may well be acceptable but the finished effect may not be quite what you hoped for.

WHERE TO LOOK

Demolition yards and specialist dealers will be able to offer selections of old flooring. A good dealer will have the flooring from each source bundled together so that there is a strong possibility that the end result will match—always assuming that the original floor has remained intact over its lifespan and not been repaired with non-matching woods.

POTENTIAL

Flooring with wear and colour makes excellent raw material for other restoration work—wide planking in either hard or soft woods can be turned into interesting walling or tabletops, for example. Do take care when buying a complete floor *in situ*. If there has been inadequate ventilation under the floorboards, wet and dry rot may have spread its way throughout the timber. Lifting a section can frequently only tell you a local story and the situation could easily be far worse (or even better) elsewhere in the floor. It is generally wiser to pay the extra price and buy from a dealer who knows something of timber and flooring and take his advice and guidance once you have told him of its eventual purpose.

RESTORATION

The restoration of floors does not present any particular problems and is perhaps easier than most as the specific rules for each particular timber apply. The hardest part of the process is the satisfactory blending and matching of the old and the replacement. If an entire floor is to be laid, it is always advisable to buy extra from the same original source and store the balance for future restoration work.

When choosing floors, it is most important to decide what the eventual purpose of the floor will be as the degree of heavy use will influence the choice. Narrow areas such as hallways and lobbies will almost certainly demand hardwood floors, larger rooms can take proportionally wider planks—generally softwood. Decide whether you will use a large central rug or carpet or smaller rugs, and if the rugs themselves are antiques, which colour of flooring will compliment their patterns and colours. Bear in mind the overall effect you wish to create—country rustic, old colonial or smart town set.

VARIATIONS

Look for sprung dance floors, parquet floors (but take care that the mastic material used in their original laying can be satisfactorily removed) the width of planks, previous use—some pitch pine wide-planked floors from the textile mills of West Yorkshire in England can retain their distinctive smell of lanolin oil for ever.

A glorious example of the beauty of wood at Manderston in the Scottish border country. Notice how a contrasting shade of wood forms a border to the floor.

DOORS

O f all the period architectural materials stocked by dealers, doors are the most numerous. Their variety and detail is virtually endless as they have found their way there from all types and ages of properties, rich and poor, domestic and business, poor-house and bank.

One important rule to bear in mind when searching for doors is to buy the doors first and make the holes to fit them rather than the other way round. It is always easier to make the space fit the door than to enlarge or reduce an existing old, and perhaps frail, door. If all else fails and you are forced to reduce the size of a door always check first of all to see if the uprights will withstand the chopping away of the timber without it weakening them too much.

If you need a number of doors for a renovation ask the dealer if he has any 'suites' all taken from the same original house or building. These suites of matching doors invariably command a premium price.

WHERE TO LOOK
A good dealer in architectural antiques should be able to offer you a good selection of period doors to suit most tastes and periods. In the case of some specialists the selection at any one time can run into literally thousands. In a good dealer they will be arranged in racks with the size clearly marked on the leading edge. In a really excellent dealer, the price will also be plainly shown.

Avoid painted doors of all descriptions unless you are especially confident or desperate to have that particular one! Paint can, as with all building materials, hide a multiplicity of sins and past brushes with red oxide preservative paint. The scorch marks caused by the over-enthusiastic application of a blow torch may also be hidden. Don't always take the dealer's word that the paint will strip off easily. If it were going to come off that easily he would probably have tackled it himself. One of the most unpleasant

surprises you may get with a painted door are plywood panels, which usually means that the door is virtually scrap, fit only for the bonfire. Take care also with old doors which have been flush finished with hardboard—all the vogue for modernization in the 1960s. In theory this should mean that the surface has been protected but it can also frequently mean that any raised-

This fine Georgian period doorway features a substantial four-panelled door, an attractive fanlight, side panelling and reeded columns.

Two fine English Georgian doorways in a classic style.

panel mouldings have either been totally removed or planed down to allow the hardboard to lay flat.

RESTORATION

Restoration of doors does not present any particular problem other than that found with other woodwork. Mahogany and oak doors are the easiest to restore without trace as these woods are usually stained and/or polished and the telltale marks can be hidden or disguised by a competent restorer. Pine is much less easy and this is important as pine doors are the commonest and also the most popular. Marks of locks, finger plates, old escutcheons, clothes hooks, and so on, all leave their tell-tale marks and may have to be filled and stained slightly to attempt to match the colour of the remainder of the door.

POTENTIAL

Victorian and even Georgian doors compare favourably in price with good quality modern doors and have the additional attraction of patina and attractive wear. As such they add considerably to the visual warmth of any old home and can work wonders for a new house decoration scheme.

Many British doors just happen to be approximately the same size as the side panel of a modern bath. This provides the opportunity of adding a charming period touch to a bathroom without the possible problems and inconveniences associated with a genuine old bath installation.

VARIATIONS

With pine doors, look for pitch pine, which is not generally highly regarded by the trade—not because there is anything wrong with it but purely for the reason that it does not sell well. This is rather unfortunate as pitch pine is one of the most beautiful of woods—second only to yew in colour, texture and grain. Also with pine doors look for the number of panels—six-panel doors are more eagerly sought after and are usually priced above four-panel ones—however a really good four-panel example is to be favoured over a poor quality six-panel specimen.

Look for fairly heavy construction, which usually indicates a door of some quality, interesting and/or heavy mouldings, beading and panelling, good colour, and most of all, original door furniture, or, at the very least, only signs of one set of furniture in the door's lifetime. Never buy a door which is slightly smaller than your existing doorway: your joiner will not want to plane and hang the door so that it is a perfect fit and then ruin it by adding packing strips to the edges.

RIGHT. These front doors were taken from a local country house which was being demolished and installed on an eighteenth-century mill building converted to domestic use.

LEFT. A cast iron urn is grouped with a Victorian cast iron park bench to frame an internal six-panel Georgian door extended to the top to fit the archway.

ABOVE. An interior view of an inner front door in stripped pine with inset panels of Edwardian period stained glass. In the foreground is a typical Victorian four-panel door.

39

WINDOWS

WHERE TO LOOK

As with all searches for architectural antiques, keep an eye open for derelict property which might be due for demolition and visit demolition dealers and the specialists who trade in recycled building materials. Make regular calls on firms who specialize in replacement metal or plastic framed windows or in double glazing. Many of them remove hundreds of perfectly sound windows each week and can be persuaded to be

Finely carved stonework surrounds an interesting window in a municipal building. Features of this type and quality can frequently be found in architectural antique dealers and can be used in a variety of decorative applications.

ABOVE LEFT.
This interesting window in Cornwall features central hinges and the window shape is mirrored by a moulding on the wall above.
LEFT. *The two central arched astragals designed by a master craftsman set this eighteenth-century classic Georgian window apart from its neighbours.*

RIGHT.
Dramatic metal-framed windows in an old railway station. It is easy to see how these could be adapted for other decorative uses should the building ever be demolished.

41

especially careful if they know you are seriously interested.

Metal windows can be very attractive in the dealer's premises but should be viewed with caution. They are difficult to re-glaze and are highly liable to sudden expansion and contraction with temperature changes, which can cause leaks and drafts. If used, do try and place them on the colder side of the building where the temperature variations are likely to be less violent. In general most window frames are made from either wood or metal. Wood frames can suffer from rot, especially along the lower edge where water has gathered over the years, but otherwise present no special problems. Look for a design you like and, if possible, alter the opening rather than the window frame.

With Georgian windows, remember that the paint was supposed to overlap slightly onto the glass and was intended to form a perfect weather seal. There is a tendency today to attempt to keep the paint purely to the woodwork and to clean off extensively right back to the end of the glass. This doesn't really help to preserve the glazing bars and is out of character for old windows.

RESTORATION
Restoration of window frame woodwork presents no particular problem for a craftsman or skilled amateur. Check to determine the exact configuration of the astragals or glazing bars when

replacing as these should have the same 'shadow lines'. These complicated mouldings give a period window its delicate appearance and finesse. If the glass dates from the early nineteenth century or earlier it will be very thin and exhibit charming blemishes and shading which contribute to the changing patterns of light and add, to a considerable extent, to the charm of old glass. If this requires replacement, the specialist architectural antiques dealer is the first place to call but a good second choice is a picture framer or an auction sale of old prints. Odd lots of old picture frames can produce a good crop of useable window glass. As most old frames had fairly small panes, picture glass is frequently close to the correct size and is simply cut.

POTENTIAL
Attractively shaped window frames, either with or without glass, can find new and attractive homes as room dividers or purely as decorative features. An early Georgian example featuring many small frames can add a new dimension on a large interior wall, frequently back-lit as in a light box.

Look for the technicalities and mechanics of window opening. If you buy a complete Georgian or Victorian window, always check to see that the sash cords and weights are in sound condition. Window cords would be best replaced in any event as failure could cause a terrible accident.

The classic dimensions of a typical example of a Venetian window in a small country house in North Yorkshire.

STAINED GLASS

The history of stained glass in England can be divided simply into three periods: the rare and beautiful medieval glass of the twelfth and thirteenth centuries; that of the Victorian revival, and, the most common glass, that of the Edwardian factories.

WHERE TO LOOK

Every Edwardian family of any social pretensions would invariably insist that a house had a vast spectrum of coloured glass. Whether a country mansion or a terraced house, the front lobby usually displayed a full compliment of illuminated glass. By far the largest collection was found there—the entire inner-door top panel would be coloured glass with further narrow panels on either side.

POTENTIAL

During the 1950s and 60s Britain enjoyed a 'modernization' period when all relics of previous eras were removed. Stained glass was replaced with numb 'obscured' glass—beautifully panelled interior doors had their mouldings ripped away and replaced with bland hardboard panels and the like. The terraced houses of the turn of the twentieth century were virtually raped by their new owners and many of the 'features' were thrown out in the rubbish.

In this period much of the discarded domestic stained glass found its way into the lower echelons of the antique trade. These traders had discovered a ready market for all types of coloured glass from more discerning customers in the United States—mainly on the West Coast. Antique entrepreneurs such as The Golden Movement in California and Andy Thornton in England solved the problem of over-supply in a brilliant way—the glass was incorporated skilfully into 'Victorian' conservatories. These were designed and constructed in England in sections which allowed them to be easily shipped across the Atlantic and then quickly re-erected and sold in specialist architectural auctions.

VARIATIONS

Most Edwardian stained glass would be of a few varying designs in, usually pale, rather insipid—dare we say 'tasteful'—tones, in stark contrast to the highly coloured examples seen in the dramatic examples from the famous glass workshops of Tiffany in New York. Birds and family armorial crests were favourite pictorial subjects for stained glass artists of the period, who mixed these illustrated panels with simple geometric shapes to form complete panels destined to find their way into inner porch doors, over-windows and even shop fronts all over the country.

There has always been a great tradition for ecclesiastical stained glass in England. Much survives today from medieval times—despite the bombing raids of the Second World War which wrought such havoc in city churches. This early glass, exemplified in the fine windows of great churches such as York Minster (which has more medieval glass than all other churches in England put together) is superb in design, depth of colour and sheer quality. Victorian glass can also be of very fine quality but the Edwardian era heralded a virtual boom in the fashion and, with production explosion, a rapid decline in colour, design and execution.

Beware of buying panels or complete windows of English church glass which has no framework. If the glass is virtually sandwiched in a timber framework ready for transport with no integral 'edging' to hold it together—be careful. These panels are highly flexible and can twist, bend and shatter very easily not only in transit but also on removal and when you attempt to install them in their new home.

RESTORATION

The restoration of stained glass of any age and

LEFT. Alaskan wild flowers incorporated in a stained glass commission by the University of Alaska from the Lyn Hovey Studio of Cambridge, Massachusetts. RIGHT. A stained glass design by the Williams Art Glass Studios of Oxford, Michigan.

RIGHT. A fine panel of Edwardian stained glass has been mounted in a contemporary pine door and used to lead into a plant filled conservatory. The large quarry tiles used on the conservatory floor echo the earth tones of the dried flower arrangement.
OPPOSITE. Old stained glass may not always fit the space available and it is then possible to commission a new work. This gives the opportunity to choose your own favourite subject and in this roundel by English stained glass artist, Anne Sotheran, the owner's pet Indian Mynah Bird is faithfully captured.

quality is, without question, best left to the expert. A wide variety of skills and disciplines are involved in fine restoration and these are certainly not picked up overnight from a textbook. If you have any difficulty locating a restorer in your locality, make contact with any local church or cathedral who boasts stained glass windows—they should be able to advise you.

LOOK FOR
Americans have always appreciated good stained glass, being influenced by the truly superb work of the famous Tiffany workshops in New York.

Genuine Tiffany glass is, however, horrendously expensive and very rare. The English imported glass presented an affordable, although technically and artistically highly inferior, substitute. The first imports were used at the decorator's every whim; set into existing windows and doors or illuminated, framed and hung as 'Victorian pictures'. In 1972 the demand was virtually insatiable and containers brimming with coloured glass literally crossed the Atlantic daily. The tap was suddenly turned off in the mid-seventies when leading influential Californian designers decreed 'No more English stained glass'.

IRONWORK

CAST IRON

WHERE TO LOOK
Apart from the usual trade sources, some of the best examples of English cast iron are to be found in railway stations, hospitals, churches and chapels as well as in many Victorian and Edwardian factories. In addition many specimens were imported from Australia at the end of the nineteenth century. In the United States there is an even stronger tradition of fine cast iron work which is lovingly preserved to this day in some of the great cities of the South.

Beware of modern cast iron and aluminium reproductions—the former are difficult to detect, the latter very easy due to their lack of weight. Most modern cast iron tables and chairs bear a maker's mark and were not produced to deceive. However these raised cast marks can be simply removed by an unscrupulous dealer and the reproductions passed off as genuine period pieces.

RESTORATION

Contrary to popular belief, cast iron is not necessarily difficult to repair or restore. The main problem is finding a craftsman willing to take the time and trouble to produce an undetectable repair. All too often, the so-called 'repair' turns out to be a disfiguring lumpy mess on the finely chiselled metalwork and can totally destroy the value and appearance of the piece. Do think twice about removing all the accrued paint of ages. The frequent thick applications of successive coats of a 'good quality oil-based paint' has resulted in the decorated cast iron becoming soft and rounded over the years. In this process it loses much of its fine detail, in the sense that this is totally obscured by the multi-layers of thick paint. It would be nice to remove the last seventy years' paint leaving, say, the first twenty years', but the action of the dip in the hot caustic-soda tank is a case of one off, all off and the metal is reduced to its pristine original condition. In this state it looks just as it did when it left the foundry, with little of the very beautiful roundness you may have admired.

One exception to the cast iron restoration rule is the spiral staircase. It is really unwise to buy an old cast iron staircase actually in its original setting. The strong possibility will exist that all the bolts will have become seriously corroded and will prove difficult, not to say impossible, to remove. This may well cause the ironwork to fracture and lead to expensive repairs. It is always worth seeking out a fully restored staircase and buying with installation as part of the contract.

POTENTIAL

You will find more cast iron in the architectural antique dealer's yard than almost anything else, with a great variety of decorative and useful applications. There is hardly a room which would not benefit from the addition of a decorated and painted bracket, grille or panel, or a larger scale cast iron fireplace complete with fire irons.

OPPOSITE. Cast iron balcony panels were once considered a sign of great elegance in British town houses and many fine examples are still to be found in London, Cheltenham, Edinburgh and other cities with a fine architectural tradition.

LEFT. Cast iron work from the foundries of Britain and the United States.

VARIATIONS

A glance around any dealer's premises will give you a taste of the endless variety of design and decorating in cast iron. It can also be fun to speculate on the original function or purpose of an odd-shaped piece and wonder what could be done with it today. It really matters little whether it started life holding up a china cistern in a gentleman's public lavatory if it will now play a supporting role in your conservatory.

Look for Victorian date triangles or makers' marks. If you are buying directly from its original home, be it church, chapel or factory, it is often possible to examine records to establish the date of manufacture and the name of the craftsman or local firm involved.

An especially fine cast iron garden seat with four illustrative plaques reputedly manufactured for the Great Exhibition of 1852.

LEFT. Cast iron balcony panels from a demolished manor house find a new home as a minstrels' gallery.

BELOW. A fine and rare pair of nasturtium pattern cast iron garden chairs made at Coalbrookdale in 1870. The original superb colour is outstanding in these examples.

The urn to the rear is a nineteenth-century example, again cast iron.

WROUGHT IRONWORK

WHERE TO LOOK

Churches and chapels are a prime source of fine old wrought ironwork. You can often discover the precise provenance of your piece as most churches keep accurate records or have enthusiastic local church historians who will be happy to assist with research. It should generally be possible to date the manufacture and, in a great many cases, the name of the craftsman responsible when you are close to the original source. If you are buying from a dealer the ironwork may have passed through several hands and its origins become clouded. Beware of overcleaning or stripping off the accrued paint. It is all too easy to subject your ironwork to a nice cleansing bath of hot caustic soda from which it will arise stripped of all the character and patina so carefully accumulated over the years.

RESTORATION

Restoration of wrought iron should be the sole province of the specialist: if a piece is worthy of restoration a specialist must be used. Surprisingly enough such specialists are not really expensive provided they do the job to your (and invariably *their*) satisfaction. An expensive restoration is the poor job which has to be done again or the one which ruins the article. A break in a piece of wrought iron would seem, at first glance, to require a quick flash with the welding torch but nothing can be further from the truth. Old wrought iron is as sensitive and responsive as eighteenth-century mahogany and should be treated with just as much care.

POTENTIAL

Wrought iron can find a new home today both inside and outside and can be attractively used, for example, as brackets or supports. Many pieces of ornamental ironwork were brightly coloured when first made and can benefit from such restoration as the gold leaf and red paint tongues on iron flowers. Such treatment can sometimes look a trifle gaudy at first but normally matures quickly.

VARIATIONS

Look for regional or national variations in wrought ironwork. There is a long tradition of English ironwork but supremely fine examples can also be bought (usually at extremely high prices) in France, Italy and Germany. Especially in Italy and Germany the tradition of the ornamental window grille has evolved.

Always look for high quality. Every writer on antiques stresses that high quality is of paramount importance. Nowhere is this more true than with wrought ironwork, but the really surprising thing is that a great many people seem unable to spot the tell-tale signs of this quality, and the variation of thickness as the metal terminates—smoothly tapering as it twists and curls.

A wrought iron Italianate wellhead, one of the most highly prized of all simple architectural antiques.

Harrogate is one of the many English towns especially renowned for its ornamental ironwork. Here we can see the distressing effect of time and the elements on a formerly glorious wrought iron balcony which may, one day, fall prey to an enterprising architectural antique dealer.

FIREPLACES

WHERE TO LOOK

There are probably more fireplace sources listed in this book than any other specialists and this reflects, to a large extent, the great interest in this part of house furnishing. There was a time in the British antique business when it was virually impossible to sell anything connected with a fireplace to a visiting American customer. Today this has changed to a great extent with the new-found popularity of the hearth, and the

LEFT. Great interest has been shown in restoring and using many of England's fine country houses as hotels of great traditional style and distinction. Using authentic materials is paramount in these restoration projects and high skilled research is essential as epitomized in this charming eighteenth-century fireplace setting at Middlethorpe Hall Hotel.

OPPOSITE. This open plan fireplace utilizes several recycled architectural features to frame the modern Swedish wood-burning stove. The bricks are all early eighteenth-century examples, cleaned and selected, then sealed with polyurethane varnish to prevent dusting; the club fender is, in reality, a church altar rail; the 'holes' in the rear wall are old land drains and allow heat to circulate and make an ideal warming place for red wine. The brass rail holding the curtain to the right is from a Victorian fireplace overmantle.

prestige of owning a fireplace.

BEWARE

Reproduction fireplaces abound in all styles, materials and periods from the classic Georgian wood chimneypieces to the cast iron copies of Victorian and Edwardian surrounds. They are mostly of good quality and the only danger is if one is passed off as the genuine article. There is

A barn in northern England under reconstruction using a variety of re-claimed achitectural fittings. The beams are pitch pine and were sold (purely by chance) in a factory under demolition. They were originally 46 feet long and were reduced to fit their new home. The doors are from local farms; the traditional Yorkist range contains a fire and numerous ovens and hot water heating boiler. The metal door set in the wall to the left of the range is a bread oven, and the aperture to the right holds a 'copper'—a huge metal tub for washing clothes.

a major danger with pine fire surrounds, which have been constructed with less-than-dry materials. When in position and operating, the heat of the fire rapidly dries out the frame which then cracks, splits and twists. If the basic frame is decorated with applied carved flowers, swags and decorations, often imported from Italy, the drying rates of the two timbers may well be different which can cause the decoration to become loose and, at worst, fall off.

RESTORATION

Timber chimneypieces require only skilled workmanship rather than particular specialist knowledge. Repairs to metal, slate, and marble slips and surrounds, obviously require specialists in their own disciplines. If the chimneypiece is painted and requires stripping, check to see if the decoration is carved wood or gesso before dipping in caustic soda. If it turns out to be the latter this may well mean that you could lose a great deal of it in the immersion process as the wood expands and contracts in the liquid but the plaster gesso does not! Care should also be taken when cleaning 'marble' fireplaces as they can often turn out to be painted slate and you will find yourself actually removing the marble!

POTENTIAL AND VARIATIONS

A fireplace is the focal point of any room and, as such, receives a great deal of attention. There is a vast selection of designs, styles and periods to choose, from the primitive inglenook to the severe and restrained classic marble and pine of Robert Adam or to the vulgarity of cast iron and marble excesses of the Victorians and Edwardians. There are examples to satisfy any taste in every architectural antique dealer and demolition yard as well as in many general antique dealers. The latter often only offer fine eighteenth-century examples in pine and marble and a selection of French and English fenders and fire irons. The proportions of English and American chimneypieces are quite different. The English style favours an upright stance, taller than it is wide usually with a ratio of seventy-five per cent to the width of the chimney breast. The classic American style is longer, lower and heavier in treatment than its old world equivalent.

Look for all the dozens of attendant accessories which can make the fireplace so interesting and a reflection of social history in general. Nearly everything connected with the fireplace has a specific purpose which is linked to the habits and practices of previous generations. Look, for instance, at the decorative tiles surrounding the metal basket grate, each one designed to tell a story for the long winter evenings without television, the numerous designs of screens to keep the heat from the mistress's delicate cheeks, the patent devices to light the fire, the mechanical bellows—the list is endless and profoundly fascinating.

BATHROOMS

WHERE TO LOOK

There are architectural dealers who specialize in complete bathrooms and also hold stocks of literally thousands of taps, showers and mixer taps, either offered in their original state, or fully restored to complete working condition and probably good for another fifty years. The best source for fittings in vast numbers is the demolition or refurbishing of an Edwardian or Victorian English hotel. If you are lucky enough to be on the spot when the work is in progress look out for some baths as well—they are likely to be absolutely huge and complete heaven to use. Many of these specialist dealers can also offer reproduction bathrooms and fittings made from the original patterns and hand painted or decorated.

Check the current building regulations before installing a genuine old bathroom, paying particular attention to the fittings and pipes. Lead pipes are now considered poisonous and the capacity of water cisterns needs checking.

RESTORATION

The restoration of working fittings, taps, shower heads and the like is for specialist restorers or, that extremely rare breed, keen and dedicated plumbers. The ideal way to ensure a trouble-free tap is to replace all the working bits and pieces inside leaving only the attractive exterior in its original state. It is worth remembering that old English and American fittings and taps were all made to imperial measurements and will not accept metric replacement parts. When buying a mixer tap set with a shower hose banded in brass spring-like material, expect it to leak—it can easily be replaced with a modern equivalent, although the brass colour may not be a totally happy match.

POTENTIAL

Because of the unusual and attractive design of many pieces of Victorian and Edwardian bathroom fittings, odd single items can find their way quite happily into other rooms. An elegant marble and brass hand basin will look equally at home in the dressing room or in the bedroom, and a travelling (possible Georgian) hand basin in a mahogany cabinet makes a useful part of a drinks cabinet.

VARIATIONS

Specialized fittings from trains and ocean liners can create an individual atmosphere for a rather special *en suite* bathroom especially if the theme is carried throughout with dark mahogany bunks and built-in cabinets and cupboards.

The most desirable items to look for are original decorated bathroom suites in perfect conditions, complete panelled bathrooms with their massive nickel-plated controls, corner wash basins, and basins and lavatories hiding away in attractive pieces of furniture, for example eighteenth-century travelling picnic toilets.

The sort of bath every antique dealer dreams of finding! The panels and pillars are in marble, and the bath itself together with all fittings is silver plated (perhaps to match the silver staircase?)

A wide choice is always a luxury when choosing any architectural additions to your home. Taps and sink fittings in their hundreds at a Sheffield architectural antique dealers' (OPPOSITE AND ABOVE). With care and perseverance in such shops you can assemble complete period bathrooms, or Edwardian toilets (LEFT).

ETHNIC ITEMS

Attempting to describe the breadth and variety of European and American architectural antiques is sufficiently difficult in itself – extending this description to cover the wealth of material from Africa and India and the far East is quite another matter.

Today the vast majority of specially collected material which could be described as

architectural in nature comes mainly from northern India, east and west Africa and parts of Indonesia.

Several European and American gallery owners make regular sorties into these hinterlands to seek out carvings, figures, deities and interesting parts of buildings to display and sell as a totally new art form. Brought back, the trophies are cleaned and polished and presented as items which can add interest and an exotic focal point to any interior decoration scheme – both modern or antique.

The main preoccupation of these gallery owners is usually for identifiable pieces of exotic architecture which can be easily incorporated into a western scheme. Such items as windows, doors, columns and brackets are especially prized and good, well executed examples can command high prices in the west.

The idea of a sophisticated gallery owner prowling amongst the ruins of a jungle temple attempting to buy native carvings or perhaps bargaining with the owner of a Rajasthan reclaimed timber yard is certainly intriguing. Many of these collectors are reticent to discuss their precise collecting methods but one, Gordon Reece, of Knaresborough in Yorkshire,

OPPOSITE. One of a pair of massive eighteenth-century capitals in carved wood from an Indian temple. Its partner is in California, forming the base of a patio table.
ABOVE LEFT. A fine example of a Rajasthan door in a geometric design decorated with polished brass and iron fittings.
LEFT. A large Indian box on display at a Knaresborough gallery, reputedly a former village jail.

asserts that many of the sellers are as conversant with the prices made in the leading western auction houses as he is, and are not adverse to producing the latest Tribal Art catalogue from Christies or Sothebys to back up their demand for realistic prices.

A group of carved Rajasthan doors and windows from the Gordon Reece gallery in Knaresborough.

RIGHT. A *fascinating group of architectural antiques awaiting final positioning at Sotheby's premises in Sussex. In the foreground is a twentieth-century Italian terracotta garden seat, the ends featuring winged grotesque creatures and a matching table. Behind the oriental stone dog stand a pair of nineteenth-century stoneware rustic garden seats, the holes designed to contain plants.*
OPPOSITE PAGE, LEFT. *A fine large pair of old terracotta garden urns decorated with lion masks.*
OPPOSITE, PAGE RIGHT. *A huge cast iron garden urn found in the tiny front garden of a house in Pontefract. It consists of a base plus fifty identical cast iron frames which quickly slot into the base and a retaining band around the rim.*

GARDEN FEATURES

WHERE TO LOOK

Architectural antiques for the garden come in a wide variety of shapes and sizes—some useful some purely decorative. Every specialist dealer in architectural antiques will be able to offer a selection, and there are dealers who specialize in little else—their stock ranging through tiny rough stone troughs to complete gazebos. Because garden antiques are usually highly visible, there is also the possibility of the 'cold call'— just stopping and asking about the urn or trough in the garden. Is it old? Where did they get it? Is it for sale? At the very worst you will get a rude rebuff or an attack by a savage guard dog. At best, an urn!

POTENTIAL

If chosen carefully, architectural antiques can add interest, variety and exciting visual focal points to any garden. Sheer scale is most important when considering any dramatic addition to a landscape. If the item is too big or is dwarfed by its new neighbours the effort and effect can be wasted. It really helps to have a photograph taken from a natural viewing point to see it the new addition will fit. If you imagine the urn next to a particular shrub, you will no doubt know the approximate size of the plant and will be able to judge the effect of the new addition. We cannot really stray into the specialist realms of garden design, but it is fair to

say that any major architectural antique introduced into any given outdoor situation is going to have a profound effect of its surroundings and it's really worthwhile considering exactly what you want before shopping around. If on the other hand you find something that you cannot resist, take it into 'stock' and live with it until the right place is found. Nothing in a garden is finite and most architectural antiques can be moved until the most satisfactory location is found.

VARIATIONS
A quick visit to any specialist dealer will demonstrate the fabulous variety of architectural items available for the garden. Urns, seats, tables, troughs, summer houses, gazebos, statues, fountains, bird baths, sundials, weather-vanes will all be represented in their stock and these are only the items *originally intended* for the garden. Add to this list all the hundreds of other objects which could make an interesting addition to the patio or terrace or just as a latter-day folly.

Beware of introducing terracotta statues or pots on a permanent basis where there is a possibility of severe frost. Following on from the remarks about visibility in the preceding section, the security of valuable architectural items in clear view can be a problem for which there is no easy remedy.

RESTORATION
Restoration is very much a matter of personal taste and has to be considered in relation to the type of garden and the effect required. A whole body of English gardening opinion would actively seek out damaged or broken garden effects and introduce these just as they are without attempting any form of restoration or repair. The underlying attempt would be to try and give the impression that the urn, trough or whatever

has been there since the garden was first created and has suffered damage during that lifetime. It adds up, if done properly, to the timelessness of the typical English garden.

The many different materials found in garden antiques all present their own particular problems, especially in relation to their exposed positions to wind, weather and frost. Lead troughs and statues will have worn thin over the years and will require careful handling. On the other end of the scale, stone troughs are extremely heavy and, for this very reason, are easily damaged when being unloaded—they should ideally be bought on a 'delivered in perfect condition' basis. This applies to scratches to their weathered surfaces as well as actual breaks. Stone troughs should always be well wrapped in sacking and are best handled only by experts with the right equipment.

Look for additions to the garden with some wear, distress, even rust—in essence, some character which will tone in with the natural existing stone and wood in its new surroundings. Nothing looks more incongruous in an established natural garden than pristine, newly painted furniture or raw stonework with no traces of moss or lichens and wear. In a totally formal town garden, perhaps, where the garden is considered part of the home outdoors, a certain order is desirable and the paintwork can, in these cases, be gleaming.

LEFT. A dramatic sandstone lidded urn, one of a pair offered at auction by Sotheby's. A full 51 inches high, they are reputed to be the work of Jan Pieter van Baurscheit the Elder in the early eighteenth century.

ABOVE. Three very different tastes: on the left a high-relief cast iron garden urn on its plinth; in the centre an erotic carving in composition stone of a wood nymph and a satyr as the centrepiece of a garden seat; to the right a white marble group of a maiden with Cupid with Giovani Battista Lombardi.

CONSERVATORIES

The fashion for Victorian (seldom 'Edwardian') conservatories started in England in earnest in the early 1970s when the influential interior magazines featured the Amdega creations of Richardson in Darlington and, a little later, Machin Designs.

One single dominant and important feature distinguishes an 'American' conservatory from its English equivalent: the frame colour. The taste in England was, and is, always for white painted wood (or, infrequently, oiled cedarwood). In the United States, the fashionable finish is dark green wood and ironwork.

White is difficult—not to say impossible—to keep clean, whereas dark green is rich and opulent and does not show grime and dirt. It

A large classical conservatory by Machin Designs of England assembled on a hill-top site in Pennsylvania where it enjoys extensive views of the gardens and grounds in all directions. The south facing aspect ensures maximum benefit from the strong sunlight which is filtered by pinoleum blinds during the summer months.

OPPOSITE PAGE. Inside, the conservatory follows the traditional idea of an entertaining area opening from the drawing room where guests can enjoy the plants in their prime brought directly from the greenhouses. A Sepik River mask adds an interesting conversation piece to this garden room in Philadelphia.

lends itself well to evening entertaining and clever lighting. The romantic atmosphere of the conservatory is further enhanced by the use of reclaimed old English stained glass which adds that extra special magic. Perhaps the best solution is dark green inside and sparkling white outside—the happiest marriage of the two worlds.

In the interior design magazines, the sophisticated conservatory supper party is usually portrayed with lush palms, cast iron furniture and interior lights. In practice, however, the most magical effects are achieved when the building is lit from overhead, *outside*. This lighting treatment has the effect of casting the most dramatic shadows and highlighting the plants and interior shadows with subtle contrasts.

If, as a native New Yorker, your idea of conservatory stained glass is the brilliantly coloured Tiffany ceilings of Maxwell's Plumb restaurant or the New York Yacht Club, you are going to be sadly disappointed with the English equivalent which invariably smells of dying plant life rather than of charcoal broiled sirloin steaks.

RESTORATION
In the conservatory which is made of timber and glass sympathetic restoration is no real problem. If specialist materials, for example curved glass or ornamental and decorative metal castings are involved, restoration is more complex and a specialist in the field in question will probably be required.

POTENTIAL
Conservatories have come full circle from the eighteenth-century vision of ornamental glazed rooms full of perfect plants brought in from propagating greenhouses and returned after they had served their particular purpose. Today they are, in the main, used as house extensions and as swimming pool enclosures.

VARIATIONS
Basic conservatory designs appear to fall into

two categories: the traditional, exemplified by the Amdega range; and the much more fanciful, beautiful and technically more advanced houses designed and built by Machin.

Look for a design which is both aesthetically satisfying and appropriate for its purpose—to house a mixture of people and plants. All too often the complexities of Victorian design create little nooks and crannies which can harbour every garden pest known to mankind. Running

costs can also play a part in choice and heating methods, heat loss, ventilation and double glazing should all be taken into consideration so that the conservatory can be used all year round.

Do take care when employing any conservatory firm which has no track record. Insist on viewing other conservatories they have designed and constructed, speak to their owners to find out if they are fully satisfied with the contract and service.

GAZEBOS & FOLLIES

Antique gazebos are possibly best bought from dealers with sufficient space or gardens to display them actually erected rather than taking the considerable risk of a collection of parts which you may be assured will transform into a thing of garden beauty. Such will frequently not be the case as the most important parts will undoubtedly be missing.

A little care should be taken when considering such a major addition to your garden landscape, as many gazebos are large by today's standards and true follies are frequently just that! Scale is all important outside as the neighbouring trees and shrubs may be dwarfed by your new piece of garden architecture. Do remember that many follies and gazebos were originally designed to be placed in a slowly evolving landscape designed to be viewed and enjoyed only from specific points and to add a classical dimension to the grounds and gardens.

RESTORATION
Total restoration could be a problem because of the possible size and the various talents required. In an ideal world, only buy such an important structure if little or no restoration is required or when you like the idea of a slowly crumbling ruin as your particular folly.

POTENTIAL
Depending upon their degree of weather-proofing, gazebos can make idyllic secret creative hiding places for artists, writers, stockbrokers and others of a sensitive and artistic temperament.

VARIATIONS
A brave landscaper can recreate a nineteenth-century-style folly using the lava stone widely sold for flower arranging. Gazebos and follies can also be created using a mixture of different materials—stone balustrading and pillars with cast iron balcony panels as basic ingredients—with a domed roof possibly adapted from a metal staircase dome.

Look for parts of gazebos—perhaps too neglected for total restoration, which can make charming ruins and carry on a fashion started in the nineteenth century with the deliberate building of classical Greek and Roman ruins in English gardens as follies.

When searching for architectural antiques in England look out for a uniquely British garden

A classical gazebo.

building—revolving summer houses which were all the rage in the twenties and thirties. Usually made of timber, these were built on metal turntables so that the French window or balcony side could be easily turned to face to sun (or shade). To recapture the correct atmosphere of the Wodehouse era, a summer house should only be used to store rotting canvas deck chairs, mouldering croquet sets and decaying cricket gear. The typical summer house, the prestige symbol of the new middle class, was never used by people. To smell the interior of an English summer house is an experience never to be forgotten.

STATUES

Statues range from superb museum pieces and acceptable examples, often brought back as souvenirs of the Grand Tour in the nineteenth century, to ghastly modern reproductions in synthetic materials or concrete. As architectural antiques statues can be of any form, human or animal, full figure or bust, complete statue or torso constructed from marble, reconstituted marble, stone, terracotta, lead or bronze.

OPPOSITE PAGE. *A pair of highly important carved stone statue groups representing* Hunting *and* Fishing *by Falconet produced circa 1783. The composition of the groups is identical to those modelled in Sevres biscuit porcelain for Louis XV.*
RIGHT. *Assorted statuary.*

WHERE TO LOOK

As a general rule, the better the dealer, the higher the quality of the statue. There are naturally exceptions to this rule but, as with all types of antique, a dealer with a good reputation will be able to advise on the quality of the purchase.

Use religious statues with some degree of care—their use in commercial situations or in a lighthearted way could be in very suspect taste and quite liable to offend. Look out for very high quality classical reproductions in reconstituted marble. This is a modern material made by mixing real marble dust with resins, and is used for moulding into complete statues and busts. The end result is very clean, totally grain free and, in a well finished example, free of tell-tale mould marks. Such statues can appear to be almost too good to be true for their usually modest price. Look also for the possibility of reflecting statues in water—many figures can be given an added dimension when placed so that they reflect in a pool or trough.

RESTORATION

By their very sculptural nature, most statues in marble, stone or lead really do demand specialist care and restoration. There is unlikely to be a listing for Statue Restoration in your local telephone directory but a call to the fine arts department of your nearest art school or college will possibly put you in touch with a sculptor interested in restoration. Straightforward restoration to plinths or bases can usually be undertaken by a monumental stonemason. When cleaning marble, pure soap and water is a good first step and can do little harm, and alcohol, acetone and benzene can also be used to remove stains. Lead or bronze should seldom be cleaned and never by an amateur, while most figures or statues destined for outside should invariably be left with their natural coat of mosses and lichens.

POTENTIAL

It may take some courage to use statues in their formal role as focal points in a garden landscape, conservatory, hall or living room. If they are used with implied importance, they must really be of first class quality otherwise the whole point of the exercise is lost and the final effect is completely pretentious. However, used purely as decorative additions or, better still, as fun, they can be quite magical and can add life and vitality to any scheme, inside or out. In a garden, statues of any sort can add focal points to a bower or avenue and can add a classical influence to a formal or wild design. If used in a formal layout, they should, perhaps, be classical in form whereas in a wild or natural garden almost any moss or lichen covered statue will suffice, provided that it looks as old and established as the surrounding vegetation. Groups of statues, for example Greek-style statues of the Four Seasons may be best used within sight of each other and formally arranged, or, in a wild garden, in charming overgrown or neglected formality.

VARIATIONS
Complete or broken statues have a charm all of their own as do simple fragments displayed with a degree of importance.

FOUNTAINS

WHERE TO LOOK

Really fine examples seem to find their own level. If you are looking for a really classic example it would pay to start at the top—at the best dealers in garden effects or architectural salvage. Considering that fountains are made up of fairly basic components—some pipes, a container to catch the water, and, of course, a statue—the price asked is often extortionate. Perhaps it's the fact that the only people with enough nerve to use a classic fountain also have the necessary finances.

Buyers should be rather careful with lead fountains, which are, by nature, very soft and easily damaged and are usually hollow, thin and consequently delicate to handle and install. They are also a ready target for the thief who will melt them down to little ingots without too many scruples.

RESTORATION

Restoration usually falls into two categories: that

BELOW and OPPOSITE. An important marble group by Camille Gresland, which features two naked Bacchantes, one playing the cymbals, the other plucking grapes from a bunch, while a putto treads grapes.

to the fabric of the fountain—the stonework, bronze or metalwork—and that to the basic plumbing—the working bits. Restoration to the fabric should not present any special problem peculiar to fountains except possibly the deterioration of metal parts due to prolonged exposure to particularly hard or acid water. A competent stonemason should be able to repair any defects or damage to that material, likewise specialist metal restorers can perform miracles to stained or damaged cast iron or bronzeworks.

Restoring the plumbing is a rather different proposition. If the complete fountain has been bought for installation then you may be able to examine all the pipes, pumps, gravity feeds,— all the elements that make the water flow. You can then have new drawings prepared for future problems and have replacement parts fabricated. If the fountain is inherited, a great deal of careful research is necessary to trace water sources and supplies before any drastic steps are taken. However, complicated as they may seem, most fountains are relatively simple in operation and most supply or pressure problems can be solved. If the supply to the fountain is found to be the culprit, perhaps the services of the local water diviner could cure the problem.

POTENTIAL
Fountains are usually found outdoors or in the conservatory and, in both situations, they can bring movement, sound and interest to any setting.

VARIATIONS
Ceramic fountains, usually from Spain or Italy are most frequently found in conservatories as their construction does not really suit severe changes in temperature. Quite often they are very bright and colourful, vividly decorated with figures and putti and can make a welcome addition to the greenery of the conservatory or orangery.

Look for colour in bronze fountains. One of the great charms to be found in antique bronze, and especially in fountains, is the action of the water and the elements on the metal turning it that unique turquoise green-blue colour. This colour follows the path of the falling water and emphasizes the carving and decoration. This colouration can be faked with small bronzes (treatment with chemicals or burial in animal urine-soaked earth are two common methods) but large pieces are unlikely to be suspect.

A superb white marble fountain featuring a naked maiden on a plinth surrounded by three bowls, again by Camille Gresland, dated 1907.

GATES

Fine wrought iron gates are possibly the definitive statement of taste and wealth among the British aristocracy. They are obviously the very first indication of the house owner's rank encountered by the visitor and will make the statement of position. Whereas the house itself may be a model of refined good taste, the main gates could just as easily be an orchestration in ironwork, bristling with curlicues and capitals, gleaming with gold leaf.

WHERE TO LOOK

Gates are invariably best bought from specialist dealers who understand their rather special qualities and requirements. Marrying a pair of wrought iron gates, hopefully complete with their overthrow, to existing gate posts is best left to an expert. Hanging gates, especially those that require alteration, are a great deal more difficult than a domestic door and every home improver knows how long *that* takes. If you could

LEFT and OPPOSITE. *The neglected charm of old wrought ironwork. Restoring the metal to its original eighteenth-century pristine condition would remove most of the subtle patterns and the feeling of growth achieved by the inroads of rust.*

BELOW. A most unusual design of field gate in bleached English oak found in a private home in North Yorkshire.

OPPOSITE PAGE. Detail of the gate illustrating the original ironwork and the attractive colour of the oak, as well as the unusual latch mechanism.

purchase the supporting posts, side railings, and all the trimmings to form a complete installation, this should, in theory at least, be a great deal simpler, and within the capabilities of the skilled amateur.

POTENTIAL
Wrought iron gates can be used to great effect both inside the home and in the more natural surroundings of the patio or garden. Gates which lead nowhere in particular are a charming feature of English garden design. Overthrows can make interesting and decorative wall decorations or features.

VARIATIONS
Most gates offered by dealers or auction houses are in wrought iron and from large estates, country houses or churches. Wooden gates are seldom for sale as they will have taken more than their fair share of work over the years and are unlikely to withstand the transition to a new home. It is always advisable to know precisely what you are looking for when you start buying. Buying for a gap in your wall or hedge without knowing the entire geography of the foundations could be fraught with problems as large iron gates are extremely heavy and the posts will consequently demand the best foundations.

RESTORATION
There should be few problems when a really first class specialist is employed. If the wrought iron gates are of some quality, their restoration is patently not a job for the local blacksmith. Locks could require the attention of an experienced locksmith and hinges could require heat treatment to free them from rust.

COMMERCIAL APPLICATIONS

Only relatively few short years ago every British brewery was ripping out all the Victorian interiors from its pubs and replacing them with 'modern' plastic and chrome monstrosities. In many respects this heralded the birth of the marketplace in architectural antiques as the local dealers recognized the intrinsic value of the solid mahogany bars, etched glass doors and panels and brass fittings. As the buildings were pulled apart the perceptive dealers stepped in and stockpiled the salvage.

WHERE TO LOOK
Today the fashion has turned full circle and Victorian-style wine bars, pubs and restaurants proliferate almost everywhere. This has created a new-found demand for the genuine article and a new breed of architectural supplier has been born. Since the trade cannot supply sufficient quantities of the old in the right size or style, many of the original suppliers have turned to producing replicas to order, a process helped in the main by the tight time scales usually involved in creating commercial premises where every day out of use means loss of profits. The demand for replicas, however, created in turn a new awareness in the old values of quality and finish and heightened appreciation of the genuine article.

COMPLETE SHOPS

Complete shops are frequently used for exciting domestic interior decoration and, more usually, for commercial applications.

WHERE TO LOOK
Architectural antique dealers and specialist auctions are the prime sources for complete shops. The other time-honoured method is just keeping your eyes open for any likely looking shop about to close or modernize. If you find a business with old shop fittings it obviously does no harm to seek out the owner and leave your name and address and hope that he might contact you if and when a sale was considered. If the business has maintained the old shop fittings there is a very good chance that the store rooms, attics and cellars are also worth more than a passing glance. It could be profitable to take along a friend in the antique business and arrange a total purchase, which could easily make the proposition more attractive from the shopkeeper's point of view.

POTENTIAL
There are fairly obvious new uses for shop fronts and interiors in wine bars and restaurants and well as in speciality shops regardless of their trade. A fine homeopathic chemists' interior from York recently became the fashionable new interior of a menswear store in Canada. On the home front the games room, den or bar could get a major rejuvenation from the addition of the walls, windows and mechanics of a *boucherie*. One of the sad facts of this recycling of shop fronts and complete interiors is that they seldom seem to end up in the same trade and are used mainly as decorators' conversation pieces.

VARIATIONS
In theory, the variety available should be as wide as trade itself but, in general, most of the complete shops offered are imported French butchers, English chemists and grocers and occasional small hand-printers. Other types of shop and shop fittings are entirely possible but their attraction would rely on their completeness and rarity. Examples that have come under the auction hammer have included a large jeweller's with really fabulous island showcases of bronze and curved glass, and a ladies' hat shop with

unique deep-drawered chests, display fittings, hat blocks and coloured fashion plates.

Beware of buying a shop in bits! Obviously the best way is to find the premises, negotiate the sale and have detailed drawings and photographs taken of all aspects of the interior. It is impossible to take too many measurements and sketches of the existing interior before dismantling. It is also highly important to discover exactly how it was constructed in the first place and, if possible, to dismantle in those same pieces or sections. Each piece should then be numbered or marked in some way and this notation marked on the master drawings. If you are offered sections of shop fittings for rebuilding, ask to see whether *they* took the trouble to itemize the pieces and sketch the original construction. Many dealers and auction houses overcome this problem by attempting to keep the shop interior (or exterior frontage) in as few parts as possible. This, as you might imagine, presents its problems but at least you will be able to see which parts are possibly missing!

RESTORATION

There are many and varied disciplines and highly skilled trades involved in shop fitting and shop interior construction and many will probably have to be sought out and involved again in the reconstruction and restoration. You could well have to become involved in the restoration of etched and stained glass, the working of fine woodwork to a standard not usually found today in other than the best antique furniture restoration workshops, the replacement or re-working of marble work surfaces, or gold leaf lettering and general gilding. Highly specialized help in connection with the specific trade or business may also be needed when unusual fittings are involved. Unlike English or American antique furniture there are no specialized dealers offering spare brass handles and fittings for shop interiors. One of the great bonuses of this aspect of architectural antiques is the fascinating research which can be still done. There is still scope for an expert in nineteenth-century English hat shops to make his mark in academia. Folk museums in many parts of the British Isles and the United States feature complete old shops with original stock and advertising and these are highly useful sources of research information.

Look for old exterior hanging shop signs and trade symbols and items of old stock which could add significantly to the appeal and display

Old architectural features find new life in commercial operations— mainly in restaurants and wine bars.

OPPOSITE. A complete French butcher's shop dismantled in Paris and imported for sale at the annual architectural antiques auction at Brillscote Farm, Gloucestershire. The shop was offered for sale complete with lettered glass signs, counters and fittings.

The wealth of variety to be found at a typical Brillscote Farm Architectural Auction—the sources ranging from British and Continental shops, gentlemen's clubs, mansions and monasteries. No possible source, it seems, is left unexplored.

The British and Continental travelling fairground or carnival has always been a source of exciting and dramatic primitive art and is appreciated by collectors and enthusiasts on both sides of the Atlantic.

The proud head is the trade sign from the complete French butcher's shop shown opposite.

Enamelled advertising signs have long been a collectors' interest and are known collectively, and charmingly, as street jewellery.

potential of a complete shop. No shop can be considered complete without stock! Contemporary advertising material and trade emphemera should also be considered for framing or display.

Pieces from shops can often find a new use in a modern home: mahogany counters, bronze and brass showcases and runs of small (sometimes decorated) drawers and decorative shelves from grocers and chemists can all look attractive. Almost any kitchen could benefit from work and preparation tables from butchers' and bakers' premises.

Architectural antiques re-used in an exciting and dramatic design for a food and beverage emporium by the Andy Thornton team from West Yorkshire who hold one of the largest stocks of architectural fittings and artifacts in Britain. The food is displayed on a backfitting salvaged from a Glasgow grocers and served from a restored dog cart.

The bar front was created using heavily detailed Gothic panelling from their architectural stockpile.

The interior of a most unusual open-plan kitchen formed in a former mill. The mill, built in 1722 to grind corn, was taken over by the famous Leeds Pottery in 1774 who installed the heavy machinery to grind flints, much of which still remains and is used to considerable dramatic effect.

INDUSTRIAL ANTIQUES

WHERE TO LOOK

The most fascinating and neglected sources for interesting architectural antiques are the workshops, mills and factories of the old industrial towns in both Britain and the United States. Many established dealers are not willing to take machinery and trade items into stock as they are frequently heavy and bulky with no proven sales record. While this means that the original sources have to be sought out, any treasures revealed and then successfully bought—it does have the enormous satisfaction of producing something very different not previously seen in this context. It also has the benefit of complete authenticity and proven provenance.

In most areas there are auction houses which specialize in the sale of factories and businesses and they will add your name to their mailing lists of commercial auctions.

POTENTIAL

Industrial material can be adapted into many situations—both domestic and commercial. Large pieces of early wooden machinery can be cleaned and polished to become industrial sculpture: interestingly shaped metalwork can be sand blasted and buffed to reveal fascinating marks and great character.

VARIATIONS

The variety of factories and workplaces which can yield interesting old architectural material with potential is, as you might suspect, endless. It is, after all, one thing finding the right factory, quite another to identify the potentially attractive or useful items, and still another to prize them loose from their present owners. From personal experience the following trades have also yielded interesting and highly unusual material.

Church organ works have provided, not altogether surprisingly, church organ pipes, many of which were extremely large and decorated. Pipes are made in metal and in square section wood which are rather less exciting and limited in use.

Printers can have large quantities of large wooden type used since the last century for poster work, and quantities of textured and worn wood. Old printing presses are much in demand as antique objects, especially early American types such as the Albion Press, which are classic examples of industrial art with gilded eagles and fruit crowning the machine. If there is a bookbinders attached to the print works this can also prove to be worth a detailed examination. The large binding presses can form the basis of an interesting group especially combined with old calf-bound ledgers and some bookbinding tools. Look for binders' sample books, which were used to illustrate the effects of the different tools.

Many of the old textile mills of the West Riding of Yorkshire are still treasure houses of architectural antiques to this day and are only slowly revealing their treasures. Giant baskets, known in the trade as 'skeps' can find new life as log containers; old wooden pattern looms are possible functional conversation pieces; buckets made from dark and shiny North American buffalo hide were brought over to England at the end of the nineteenth century and can be put to new uses in today's homes as containers for flowers or magazines. The cloth checking rooms in some textile mills can also yield superbly polished mahogany work tops which can be re-used as high quality raw material.

Flour mills have their share of large scale water-driven machinery, cogs and shafts as well as grinding stones and pulleys. Iron foundries may have pattern-making shops and stores where the three-dimensional records of their past work are stored waiting to be rescued by architectural antique enthusiasts.

Cooperages have a wide range of unique

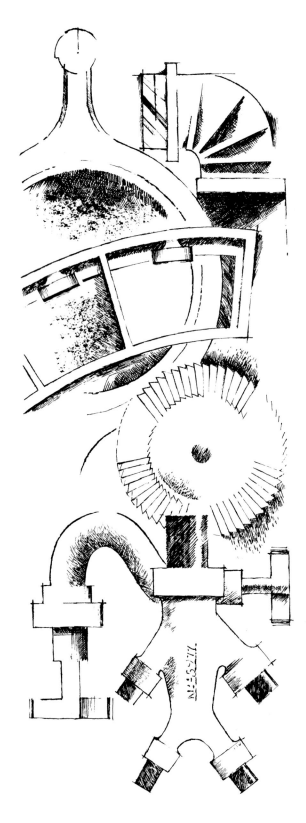

tools, (especially strangely shaped curved wood planes), iron basket fires and machinery for the manufacture of barrels, and shoemakers often have huge stocks of wooden shoe lasts from clients long since deceased. Cutlery works and ammunition factories have both proved to be interesting sources in the past although they, quite naturally, do not come on the market every day! Many old established shipbuilders may still have their mould lofts filled with platers' half ship models, as unlike modern reproductions as chalk from seasoned stilton.

Many old factories and mills proudly boasted huge tower clocks which have long since ceased to work. The factory owners may not be willing to part with the faces but the works themselves are the really choice parts and are display pieces in their own right.

A certain amount of discretion is always required when attempting to buy in factories and workplaces as the current owners will not realize the potential in everyday things they have used most of their working life. They might consider you slightly deranged as you try to buy what they consider old scrap machinery.

Do take care when buying materials or machinery *in situ* without being quite sure that they can be removed safely and reasonably easily. Transport, labour and insurance are all factors which should be considered when buying and removing from the prime source.

RESTORATION

Various effects can be achieved in metal or wood polishing using heavy duty high-speed buffing machines and metal polishing compounds. Timber is frequently burned or attractively scorched on the surface and also achieves a deep shine. Metalwork can be painted with black paint before polishing, the buffing machine achieving a pewter-like sheen on the raised parts and surfaces, the pits and blemishes remaining black thus emphasizing the character of the metal.

The potential here is really in the eye of the beholder—there is no dealer of taste and discretion to guide you along the right path if you are buying at the grass roots. Look at everything at least twice—try to imagine it divorced from its present surroundings, painted, cleaned, or polished. If the factory has been in operation for more than, say, seventy or eighty years, there really must be something interesting and exciting inside—and that's a promise!

OPPOSITE PAGE. Wooden patterns from iron and steel foundries frequently appear in auctions of architectural artifacts and are an interesting and useful addition to some interior decoration schemes.

LEFT. Genuine old architectural fittings have been skillfully incorporated into this servery area in a new English pub created by the Andy Thornton team from West Yorkshire who hold one of the largest stocks of architectural fittings and artifacts in Britain.

AN ARCHITECTURAL ANTIQUE AUCTION

With the growth in interest in architectural antiques in the past few years specialist firms have not been slow to follow and, in some cases, set the trends and style of the business. The most important specialist auctions certainly started in the United States with people such as the Golden Movement Emporium in California setting the early pace with mammoth annual auctions which attracted big names and corresponding big prices. Today the market is concentrated in a few highly organized auction houses who scour the countryside and demolition sites amassing material for either bi-

annual or annual sales where the fruits of their collections are offered for sale together with material provided by trade and private sources. This type of auction, where the vast majority of the goods on offer is actually owned by the auctioneers should, perhaps, be treated with a certain degree of circumspection.

The major British auction houses like Sothebys and Christies frequently hold specialist sales – usually combined with or concentrating on garden material which is appropriate to the style and grandeur of their country house auctions.

Quite naturally, architectural antiques will be frequently found in almost every collective sale taking place daily in nearly every town in Britain or the United States but usually in such limited variety as not, perhaps, to be specifically mentioned in the sale advertisements. Checking out every saleroom on the off chance that something interesting may be included cannot be cost-effective and buying on a private basis might well be best confined to patronizing dealers who can offer a variety of styles and sizes under one roof. Exceptions would naturally be the specialized architectural auction sales when the illustrated catalogue – which should also contain full sizing details of lots – can be studied fully well in advance.

OPPOSITE. A selection of terracotta chimney pots and plinths are dwarfed by a dramatic bronze bust of Napoleon's General Francois Marie Casimir Negrier at a Wiltshire architectural antique auction. LEFT. The same auction includes vintage aircraft propellers, chemists' drawers, a Georgian birdcage, decorated chemists' jars and enamelled tea tins. The desk style object is a chapel repair fund collection box.

TALKING POINTS

ABOVE. Carved wood carousel horses, long time favourites in the antique trade. OPPOSITE and LEFT. A 'set' of four pierced metal ceiling roses found in a country dealer's shop, which turned out to have been decorative ventilators in a Victorian chapel. They were subsequently used as window grilles and as a garden table on an old cast iron base.

These original porches, which date back to the 1900s still exist in a parade in the spa town of Harrogate. (RIGHT) A similar pine porch (BELOW), stripped of eighty years' of paint finds new life as an interesting bed canopy trimmed with heavy glazed cotton.

The Commandment panel which acts as a head board is from a Welsh church, The small chair is made from old sewing thread bobbins and probably dates from 1890.

ABOVE, LEFT. A large coffee table with an armoured plate glass top. The intricate ironwork is by Yorkshire blacksmith Chris Topp, and almost grasps the freshwater driftwood. The ceramic obelisks are by Roger Michelle. The model sailing ship is a fine late eighteenth-century merchantman, and the elephant's foot on the floor holds a collection of dried tropical fungi.

BELOW, LEFT. Fairground carousel horses dominate the foreground in this auction, together with a collection of interesting pieces of carved wood, pierced cast iron and columns in the background.

ABOVE, LEFT.
*Weathervanes –
the American art
form.* ABOVE,
RIGHT.
*Insurance signs
which once
adorned every
building of
importance.*
RIGHT. *Lanterns
in a variety of
styles.*

A nineteenth-century copy of an eighteenth-century original chimneypiece removed from a country house and inserted during a major reconstruction of an imposing York house. The middle panel of the chimneypiece, originally rather bland, was removed and the new, specially commissioned panel bearing the family's crest and initials, inserted in its place.

UK SOURCES

[Free brochures and photographs for specific requests are available from these suppliers]

ARCHITECTURAL SALVAGE SOURCES

The Antique Trader
357 Upper St, Camden Passage,
London N1
Telephone: 01 359 2019

Architectural Antiques
56 Stokes Croft, Bristol 1
Telephone: 0272 424257
Specialities: architectural salvage and artifacts

Architectural Recycling Co
Craig Hall, Rattray, Blairgowrie,
Perthshire PH10 7JB
Telephone: 0250 4749
Specialities: bathroom fittings, fireplaces, doors, spiral and straight staircases, panelling, lights, bookcases and garden furniture, mantelpieces, statuary, urns, gazebos, loggias and balustrading, flagstones

Architectural Heritage of Cheltenham
Taddington Manor, Taddington,
Nr Cutsdean, Gloucestershire
GL54 5RY
Telephone: 0242 680741
(0242 22191 evenings)
Specialities: complete rooms in period oak, Victorian oak rooms either full height or to dado height, eighteenth- and nineteenth-century pine panelled rooms, nineteenth-century mahogany panelling, doors in singles or suites, in oak mahogany and pine, chimneypieces in carved pine or oak, marble and slate, Victorian and Edwardian shop, hotel and pub interiors and exteriors and

fittings, stained and etched glass, bathroom fittings, garden statuary, carved stone, fountains, columns, corbels, bosses and pediments, cast iron balconies, verandahs, pillars, garden seats, floor boards, light fittings, decorative plasterwork

Bailey's Architectural Antiques
The Engine Shed, Ashburton
Industrial Estate, Ross-on-Wye,
Herefordshire HR9 7BW

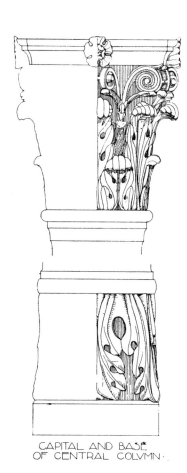

CAPITAL AND BASE
OF CENTRAL COLVMN·

Telephone: 0989 63015

Beacon Architectural Salvage
The Old School, Alderminster, Nr
Stratford-upon-Avon,
Warwickshire CV37 8NY
Telephone: 0789 87616
Specialities: old reclaimed fireplaces and doors. Open on Fridays, Saturdays and Sundays

Brighton Architectural Salvage
33 Gloucester Rd, Brighton
Telephone: 0273 681656
Specialities: period fireplaces and surrounds in marble, also pine, mahogany and cast iron. Victorian tiled and cast inserts and overmantels, doors, stained glass, decorative ironwork, light fittings and garden furniture

Bromley Demolition
75 Siward Rd, Bromley,
Kent BR2 9JY
Telephone: 01 464 3610
Specialities: basic architectural salvage, bricks, timber, tiles

Andre Busek Architectural Antiques
Savoy Show Room, New Rd,
South Molton, Devon EX36 4BH
Telephone: 07695 3342
Specialities: Georgian and Victorian fireplaces, light fittings, woodwork, furniture, bathrooms, stonework, doors, advertising items, complete panelled rooms, bars and restaurant fittings, garden items, windows and stained glass, metalwork and ironwork
Restoration: Victorian bars and fittings, light fixtures and marble fireplaces

Cantabrian Antiques and Architectural Furnishings
16 Park St, Lynton, North Devon
Telephone: 0598 53282
Specialities: general range of architectural antiques—fireplaces, doors, panelling, staircases and handrails, bathroom fittings, etched and stained glass, pub and shop fittings, oak beams
Restoration: stripping, staining, metal polishing and repair, marble restoration arranged

Alfred G Cawley & Sons Ltd
Havering Farm Cottage, Guildford
Rd, Worplesdon, Surrey GU4 7QA
Telephone: 0483 232398
Specialities: basic architectural salvage, bricks, timber, tiles

Chancery Antiques
8/10 Barrington St, Tiverton,
Devon EX16 69U
Telephone: 0884 252 416
Specialities: oak and pine country furniture and architectural items
Restoration: oak and country furniture

Cheshire Brick and Slate Co
Brookhouse Farm, Salters Bridge,
Parvin Sands, Chester CH3 8HL
Telephone: 0829 40883
Specialities: conservation, building materials and architectural antiques

Clifton Nurseries Ltd
5a Clifton Villas, Warwick
Avenue, London W9 2PH
Telephone: 01 289 6851
Specialities: antique garden ornaments and statuary, garden and conservatory furniture

G Collins
25 Cowbridge, Hertford,
Hertfordshire SH14 1GP
Telephone: 0992 582113
Restoration: old buildings, strip
and polish pine furniture, doors

Conservation Buildings Products Ltd
Forge Works, Forge Lane, Cradley
Heath, Warley, West Midlands
B64 5AL
Telephone: 0384 69551/64219
Specialities: recycling old building
materials to new sympathetic
projects, e.g. using bricks from
Victorian terraced houses to
build new farm houses and pubs,
recycling bricks from an old forge
to renovate Aston Hall in
Birmingham

John Creed Antiques Ltd
Camden Passage, London N1
Telephone: 01 607 5381
Specialities: architectural salvage
and artifacts

Daniels House
Hogshill St, Beaminster, Dorset
DT8 3AG
Telephone: 0308 862635
Specialities: architectural salvage
and artifacts

The English Street Furniture Co
Somers House, Linkfield Corner,
Redhill, Surrey RH1 1BB
Telephone: 0737 60986
US office:
3076a Via Alicante, La Jolla,
California CA 92037
Telephone: (714) 452 5863
Specialities: cast iron street lamps
and solid copper gas lanterns,
genuine telephone boxes which
have been used in a number of
ways e.g. as shower cubicles,
indoor gardens

Floyd's Builders Merchants
349 Ilderton Rd, London
SE15 1NW
Telephone: 01 639 6991
Specialities: basic architectural
salvage, bricks, slates, tiles and
timber

Genges Farm
Lymington, Ilchester, Somerset

SOFFITE OF CORONA OF PEDIMENT.

PRINCIPAL ENTABLATURE

CAP

⅛ᵗ PLAN OF CAP

⅛ᵗ PLAN OF BASE

16 FEET

BASE

DETAIL OF NICHE

PANEL

SCALE

FEET
1 METRE

BA22 8EH
Telephone: 0935 840464
Specialities: architectural salvage and artifacts

Glover and Stacey Ltd
Malthouse Premises, Main Rd, Kingsley, Nr Bordon, Hampshire
Telephone: 04203 5754
Specialities: oak beams, chimneypieces and inserts, stained glass, flooring, stair accessories, panelling, gates and ironwork, stone statues, all manner of architectural salvage. Conservatories, porticoes, fanlights and windows, paving. Projects include salvage from Windsor Castle Barracks, Brighton Pier, Hampton Court and York Minster
Restoration: manufacture of replica period fixtures and fittings in old materials—e.g. dressers, chimneypieces, bookcases, kitchens

Havenplan's Architectural Emporium
The Old Station, Station Rd, Killamarsh, Nr Sheffield, South Yorkshire S31 8EN
Telephone: 0742 489972

Hay Galleries Ltd
4 High Town, Hay-on-Wye, Herefordshire HR3 5AE
Telephone: 0497 820356
Specialities: architectural salvage and artifacts

Hayes Newby Architectural Salvage
The Pit, 70 Hare Lane, Gloucester
Telephone: 0452 31145
Specialities: preservation of church and chapel interiors

Horse Yard Antiques
67 Essex Rd, Islington, London N1
Telephone: 01 359 5730
Specialities: reclaimed fireplaces, doors, pine stripping service

The House Hospital
68 Battersea High St, London SW11
Telephone: 01 223 3179
Specialities: doors, marble and timber fireplaces, grates, baths, basins, WCs, garden railings

Hutton and Rostion Architects
Netley House, Gomshall, Nr Guildford, Surrey GU5 9QA
Telephone: 048 641 3221

Langham Architectural Materials
Langham Farm, East Nynehead, Wellington, Somerset TA21 0DD
Telephone: 0823 46297

London Architectural Salvage and Supply Co (LASCO)
St Michael's Church, Mark St, Off Paul St, London EC2A 4ER
Telephone: 01 739 0448/9
Specialities: original chimneypieces and fireplace furniture, old pine and oak panelled rooms, garden furniture, kitchen and bathroom furniture, period doors and brass foundry

M & A Main
The Old Smithy, Cerrig-Y-Drudion, Nr Corwen, North Wales LL21 9SR
Telephone: 049 082 491
Specialities: 16,000 square feet of reclaimed fireplaces, cast iron fireplaces, slates, kitchen ranges, pews, panelling, newels, spindles, handrails, architraves, mouldings, reclaimed timber, stained glass, taps, period brassware, cast iron railings, balusters, balconies, doors (both four and six panel)

Milverton Antiques
Fore St, Milverton, Taunton, Somerset TA4 1JU
Telephone: 0823 400597
Specialities: architectural salvage and artifacts

B Olds
Rear of 89 Loampit Vale, Lewisham, London SE13
Telephone: 01 692 9560

The Original Choice
1340 Stratford Rd, Hall Green, Birmingham B28 9EH
Telephone: 021 778 3821
Specialities: fireplaces, stained glass, tiles, fenders, mirrors, lampshades, garden furniture, doors, baths and staircases

Paris Ceramics
543 Battersea Park Rd, London SW11 3BL
Telephone: 01 228 5785
Specialities: terracotta floor tiles

Pine Country
14 Springvalley Gardens, Morningside, Edinburgh
Telephone: 031 447 5795
Specialties: architectural salvage and artifacts

The Pine Mine
100 Wandsworth Bridge Rd, London SW6
Telephone: 01 736 1092

Posterity Architectural Effects
Baldwins Farm, Newent, Gloucestershire GL18 1LS
Telephone: 0531 85597

DS & AG Prigmore
Mill Cottage, Mill Rd, Colmworth, Bedford MK44 2NU
Telephone: 023 062 264
Specialities: all types of demolition, specialists in reclaimed building materials, oak beams, block flooring, stone, bricks, paving, slates, tiles. Handmade bricks imported from Sri Lanka and Holland and marble lime paving from India

R & R Reclamation
Bridge St, Brigg, South Humberside DN20 8LP
Telephone: 0652 57650
Specialities: Victorian, Georgian and Tudor reclaimed bricks, crown chimney pots, pine doors and architectural features. Projects have included discovering a Tudor cottage beneath a Victorian farmhouse

Regent Supplies Ltd
Swans Rd, Cambridge
Telephone: 0223 314114

Rogers Demolition and Dismantling Service
Belgrave Rd, Portswood, Southampton
Telephone: 0703 449173
Specialities: basic architectural salvage, bricks, timber, tiles

Scallywag
187 Clapham Rd, Stockwell, London SW8
Telephone: 01 274 0300
Specialities: architectural salvage and artifacts

Sheffield Architectural Antiques
Ponds Forge, Sheaf St, Sheffield
Telephone: 0742 586480
Specialities: fireplaces, bathroom suites, panelling and stained glass, garden furniture and ornaments, doors and cast iron work, pine stripping service

Solopark Ltd
The Old Railway Station, Station Rd, Pampisford, Cambridgeshire CB2 4HB
Telephone: 0223 834663

Southbridge Building Supplies Ltd
Vowels Lane, Kingscote, East Grinstead, West Sussex RH19 4LD
Telephone: 0342 313244
Specialities: basic architectural salvage, bricks, timber, tiles

Stowaway (UK) Ltd
2 Langton Hill, Horncastle, Lincolnshire LN9 5AH
Telephone: 06582 7445
Specialities: stripping and refurbishing pine furniture and architectural items, e.g. doors, fireplace surrounds and panelling

Swanbridge Art Co
Tower Rd, Glover West Industrial Estate, District 11, Washington, Tyne and Wear NE37 2SH
Telephone: 091 415 0080
Specialities: architectural antiques for theme pub interiors

Sussex Demolition
Station Goods Yard, Hoskins Rd, Oxted, Surrey RH8 9HT
Telephone: 08833 5413
Specialities: building materials, fire surrounds, doors and brass fittings

ROYAL·ENTRANCE·LOGGIA

CLOCK COVRT
HAMPTON-COVRT PALACE.

DETAILS OF HERALDIC SCVLPTVRE.
& VASES ON BALVSTRADE.

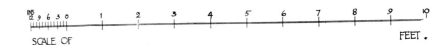

Stone Details.

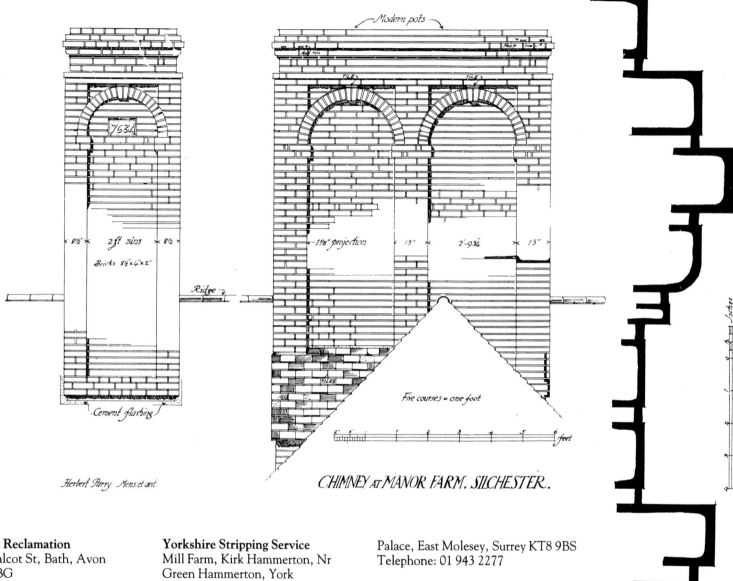

Herbert Parry *Mens.et delt.*

CHIMNEY at MANOR FARM, SILCHESTER.

Walcot Reclamation
108 Walcot St, Bath, Avon
BA1 5BG
Telephone: 0225 66291
Specialities: architectural antiques,
    traditional building materials

Wilcock and Booth
42 Elcho St, London SW11 4AU
Telephone: 01 228 3601

Woodstock (Totnes) Ltd
Station Rd, Totnes, Devon
TQ9 5JG
Telephone: 0803 864610

Woolaway and Sons
Junction Yard, Barnstable, Devon
DX31 2AE
Telephone: 0271 74191

Yorkshire Stripping Service
Mill Farm, Kirk Hammerton, Nr
Green Hammerton, York
Telephone: 0901 30451
Restoration: stripping and
    restoration of old pine

ASSOCIATIONS
AND INFORMATION
SOURCES

Ancient Monuments Society
St Andrews-by-the-Wardrobe,
Queen Victoria Street, London
EC4V 5DE
Telephone: 01 236 3934

The Building Conservation Trust
Apartment 39, Hampton Court

Palace, East Molesey, Surrey KT8 9BS
Telephone: 01 943 2277

The Civic Trust
17 Carlton House Terrace, London
SW1Y 5AW
Telephone: 01 930 0914

Colleyweston Stone Slaters Trust
61 High Street, St Martin's,
Stamford, Lincolnshire PE9 2LQ
Telephone: 0780 52075

The Georgian Group
37 Spital Square, London E1 6DY
Telephone: 01 377 1722

**Guild of Architectural
Ironmongers**
8 Stepney Green, London E1 3JU
Telephone: 01 790 3436

The Guild of Master Craftsmen
Publications Co
166 High St, Lewes, East Sussex
BN7 1YE
Telephone: 0273 477374

The Historic Buildings and
Monuments Commission
Fortress House, 23 Savile Row,
London W1X 1AB
Telephone: 01 734 6010

The National Trust
36 Queen Anne's Gate, London
SW1H 9AS
Telephone: 01 222 9251

The National Trust for Scotland
5 Charlotte Square, Edinburgh
EH2 4DU
Telephone: 031 226 5922

North Wales Quarries Association
Bryn Llanllechid, Bangor,
Gwynedd L57 3LG
Telephone: 0248 600476

The Scottish Office
Scottish Development
Department, Historic Building
Branch, 20 Brandon St, Edinburgh
EH3 5RA
Telephone: 031 556 8400

The Society for the Protection of
Ancient Buildings
37 Spital Square, London E1 6DY
Telephone: 01 377 1722

The Victorian Society
1 Priory Gardens, Bedford Park,
London W4 1TT
Telephone: 01 994 1019

The Welsh Office
Conservation and Land Division,
Brunel House, Fitzalan Rd, Cardiff
Telephone: 0222 465511

BATHROOMS

Architectural Heritage of
Cheltenham
Taddington Manor, Taddington,
Nr Cutsdean, Gloucestershire
GL54 5RY
Telephone: 0242 680741
(0242 22191 evenings)

Bailey's Architectural Antiques
The Engine Shed, Ashburton
Industrial Estate, Ross-on-Wye,
Herefordshire HR9 7BW
Telephone: 0989 63015

Andre Busek Architectural
Antiques
Savoy Show Room, New Road,
South Molton, Devon EX26 4BH
Telephone: 07695 3342

Cantabrian Antiques and
Architectural Furnishings
16 Park St, Lynton, North Devon
Telephone: 0598 53282

The House Hospital
68 Battersea High St, London SW11
Telephone: 01 223 3179

London Architectural Salvage and
Supply Co
St Michael's Church, Mark St, Off
Paul St, London EC2A 4ER
Telephone: 01 739 0448/9

M & A Main
The Old Smithy, Cerrig-Y-
Drudion, Nr Corwen, North Wales
LL21 9SR
Telephone: 049 082 491

The Original Choice
1340 Stratford Rd, Hall Green,
Birmingham B28 9EH
Telephone: 021 778 3821

Posterity Architectural Effects
Baldwin's Farm, Newent, Gloucs
GL18 1LS
Telephone: 053 185 597

Sheffield Architectural Antiques
Ponds Forge, Sheaf St, Sheffield
Telephone: 0742 586480

Au Temps Perdu
5 Stapleton Road, Old Market,
Bristol BS5 0QR
Telephone: 0272 555223

BRICKS— HANDMADE AND TRADITIONAL

Architectural Landscape Designs
3/5 Kelsey Park Rd, Beckenham

BR3 2LH
Telephone: 01 658 4455
Specialities: reclaimed bricks, clay
pantiles, Welsh slates

Blockleys Plc
Sommerfeld Road, Trench Lock,
Telford TF1 4RY
Telephone: 0952 51933

Blue Circle Bricks
Blue Circle Industries Plc, Church
Rd, Murston, Sittingbourne, Kent
ME10 3TN
Telephone: 0795 21066

Bovingdon Brickworks Ltd
Pudds Cross, Ley Hill Rd,
Bovingdon, Nr Hemel Hempstead,
Hertfordshire HP3 0NW
Telephone: 0442 833176/832575
Specialities: manufacture and
supply of various handmade
bricks in colours and sizes to
work in conservation areas,
together with early brick designs.
Projects include work on the
Chapter House in St Albans
Cathedral

Branxstone
Branxholme Industrial Estate,
Bradford Rd, Bailiff Bridge,
Brighouse, West Yorkshire
HD6 4EA
Telephone: 0484 721044
Specialities: rustic slate, Cornish
silver grey slate, redressed stone,
Westmorland slate, handmade
bricks, fireplace stone, marble

Brickwork Renovation
69 Durrington Rd, Clapton,
London E5
Telephone: 01 986 1961

The Bulmer Brick and Tile Co Ltd
Brickfields, Bulmer, Sudbury,
Suffolk CO10 7EF
Telephone: 0787 29 232

Butterley Building Materials Ltd
Wellington St, Ripley, Derbyshire
DE5 3DZ
Telephone: 0773 43661

Cheshire Brick and Slate Co
Brookhouse Farm, Salters Bridge,
Parvin Sands, Chester CH3 8HL

Telephone: 0829 40883
Specialities: conservation, building
materials and architectural
antiques

Conservation Building Products
Ltd
Forge Works, Forge Lane, Cradley
Heath, Warley, West Midlands
B64 5AL
Telephone: 0384 69551/64219
Specialities: finials, tiles, slates,
bricks, quarry tiles fireplaces

Freshfield Lane Brickworks Ltd
Freshfield Lane, Danehill,
Haywards Heath, West Sussex
RH17 7HH
Telephone: 0825 790350

Genuine Period Brick Co Ltd
Clawddnewydd, Ruthin, Clwyd
LL15 2NB
Telephone: 082 45 285
Specialities: reclaimed period
bricks, Victorian and older,
manufacture of handmade
bricks. Projects include
reclaimed bricks for renovation
of Liverpool docks and the
Ironbridge Gorge Museum at
Telford

Keymer Handmade Clay Tiles
Nye Road, Burgess Hill, West
Sussex RH15 0LZ
Telephone: 04446 2931

W T Lamb & Sons Ltd
52 East St, Horsham, West Sussex
RH12 1HN
Telephone: 0403 66201

Northcot Works Ltd
Blockley, Nr Moreton-in-Marsh,
Gloucestershire GL56 9LH
Telephone: 0386 700551
Specialities: machine and
handmade bricks of traditional
character

R & R Reclamation
Bridge St, Brigg, South
Humberside DN20 8LP
Telephone: 0652 57650
Specialities: reclaimed bricks,
Yorkshire slabs, pantiles, quarry
tiles, oak and pine doors,
fireplaces

Redland Bricks Ltd
Graylands, Horsham, Sussex
RH 12 4QG
Telephone: 0403 61161

Streetley Brick and Tile Ltd
P O Box 3, Brampton Hill,
Newcastle, Staffordshire ST5 0QU
Telephone: 0782 615381

Swanage Brick and Tile Co Ltd
Godlingstone, Swanage, Dorset
BH19 3DH
Telephone: 0929 422257
Specialities: handmade facing
bricks, Georgian and Tudor
facings, paving bricks and
Roman floor tiles

Walcot Reclamation Ltd
108 Walcot St, Bath, Avon
BA1 5BG
Telephone: 0225 66291

S F Walker
24 Fiddlebridge Industrial Centre,
Lemsford Road, Hatfield
Hertfordshire
Telephone: 07072 68857

Westbrick Ltd
Pinhoe, Exeter EX4 8JT
Telephone: 0392 66561

COMMERCIAL

Brillscote Farm Auctions
Brillscote Farm, Lea, Malmesbury,
Wiltshire
Telephone: 0666 82232
London office at:
127 St Pancras Road, London
NW1
Telephone: 01 388 2691/01 387
6039

CONSERVATORIES

Amdega Ltd
Faverdale, Darlington, Durham
DL3 0PW
Telephone: 0325 468522
Specialities: hand-built red cedar
Victorian or traditionally
designed conservatories built in
modular form for simple on site
construction, aided by the latest
in computer design equipment to
provide energy efficient conservation

**Alexander Bartholomew
Conservatories Ltd**
277 Putney Bridge Rd, London
SW15 2PT
Telephone: 01 785 7263

The Chelsea Gardener
125 Sydney St, London SW3 6NR
Telephone: 01 352 5656

**Cochrane, Flynn-Rogers and
Williams**
122 South Circular Rd, Dublin 8,
Eire
Telephone: 01 (Eire) 784174
Also at: Roden House, Dundalk
Telephone: 042 33623
Specialities: superbly elegant
conservatories designed on the
principles of the curvilinear glass
houses of the nineteenth-century
Irish iron master, Richard
Turner. Today these structures
are made of curved steel and
transparent plastics but have lost
little in their translation. Alfred
Cochrane and Jeremy Williams
also design curved steel garden
temples and ornaments
Restoration: replacing cast iron
and glass with curved steel clad
with aluminium and replacing
curved glass with shaped Lexan
to preserve original
configurations

Cranford Conservatories Ltd
Unit 8, Sankey Bridge Industrial
Estate, Liverpool Rd, Warrington
WA5 1QQ
Telephone: 0925 574574
Specialities: hand crafted
cedarwood conservatories

David Flemming Conservatory Co
Holly Oak House, 98 Knights Rd,
Bearwood, Bournemouth, Dorset
BH11 9SY
Telephone: 0202 570232

Frost & Co
The Old Chapel, Shortmead St,
Biggleswade, Bedfordshire
Telephone: 0767 312516

Gardenvase Ltd
Unit 16c, Chalwyn Industrial
Estate, St Clements Road, Poole,
Dorset BH15 3PE
Telephone: 0202 733001

Hadrian Conservatories
8/10 Button Mill Estate,
Stonehouse, Stroud,
Gloucestershire GL10 2BB
Telephone: 045 382 6459

Halls Traditional Conservatories
Halls Homes and Gardens Ltd

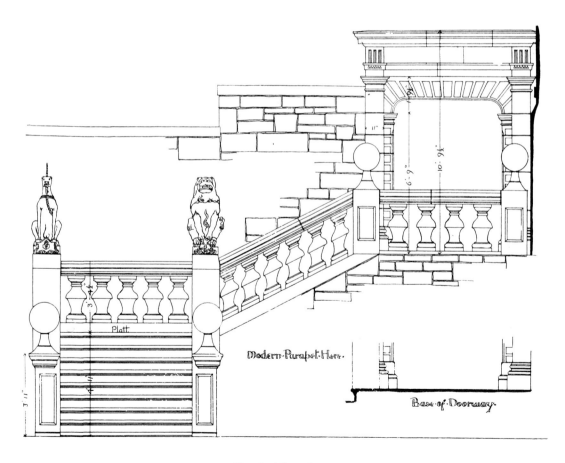

Front Elevation.

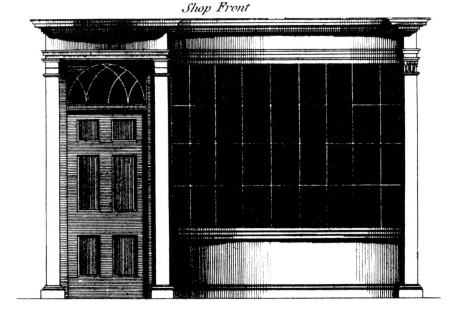

Shop Front

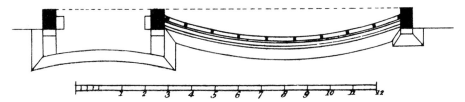

Shop Front

Church Rd, Paddock Wood, Kent
Telephone: 089 283 4444
Specialities: traditional style
British conservatories in
cedarwood, built on a cost saving
modular system which enables
the customer to choose a
conservatory to suit his exact
needs

Imperial Conservatories Ltd
Watling Rd, Bishop Auckland, Co
Durham DL14 9AU
Telephone: 0388 609668

M D Kidby Buildings Ltd
28 Kennylands Rd, Sonning
Common, Reading RG4 9JT
Telephone: 0734 723380

Machin Designs Ltd
Ransome's Dock, Parkgate Rd,
London SW11 4NP
Telephone: 01 350 1581
Specialities: the most elegant
conservatories produced in
Britain today, classically
beautiful and highly efficient,
making maximum use of modern
technology and materials

Marston and Langinger Ltd
Hall Staithe, Fakenham, Norfolk
NR21 9BW
Telephone: 0328 4933
Specialities: conservatories,
furniture in willow and cast iron

Newcroft Designs Ltd
Unit 9, Sheddingdean Industrial
Estate, Burgess Hill, West Sussex
RH15 8QY
Telephone: 04446 47684

Priory Victoriana Conservatories
Unit D, Victoria Mills, Manchester
Rd, Droylsden, Manchester
M35 6EQ
Telephone: 061 370 7112
Specialities: mahogany and
Swedish redwood conservatories

Room Outside Ltd
Goodwood Gardens, Goodwood,
Nr Chichester, West Sussex
PO18 0QB
Telephone: 0243 776563/773593
Specialities: traditional English
conservatories, restoration of

113

important old conservatories including that in the walled garden at Arlington House, Bideford for the National Trust

Town and Country Conservatories
53 Ellington St, London N7 8PN
Telephone: 01 609 9919

Vergecane Joinery Ltd
St Brelades, Jenkins Hill, London Rd, Bagshot, Surrey
Telephone: 0276 75414
Specialities: individual architecturally designed conservatories

DOORS AND DOOR FURNITURE

Architectural Components Ltd
4–10 Exhibition Rd, London SW7 2HF
Telephone: 01 581 2401
Specialities: English period door furniture

The Barewood Co
58 Mill Lane, West Hampstead, London NW6
Telephone: 01 435 7244
Specialities: original Victorian and Edwardian doors

Beardmore Architectural Ironmongery
3–5 Percy St, London W1P 0EJ
Telephone: 01 637 7041

Brass Tacks Hardware Ltd
50–54 Clerkenwell Rd, London EC1M 5PS
Telephone: 01 250 1971

Comyn Ching Ltd
19 Shelton St, Covent Garden, London WC2H 9JN
Telephone: 01 379 3026

Conservation Building Products Ltd
Forge Works, Forge Lane, Cradley Heath, Warley, West Midlands B64 5AL
Telephone: 0384 69551/64219

Specialities: pine doors, oak trusses, finials

Corrodoor Ltd
Medusa House, 249 Putney Bridge Rd, London SW15 2PU
Telephone: 01 788 8866

Danico Brass Ltd
31 Winchester Rd, Swiss Cottage, London NW3 2NR
Telephone: 01 586 7398

Erebus Ltd
377 Lichfield Rd, Wednesfield, Wolverhampton, West Midlands WV11 3HD
Telephone: 0902 737282

Grandisson Doors
The Old Hall, West Hill Rd, West Hill, Ottery St Mary, Devon EX11 1TP
Telephone: 040 481 2076
Specialities: all types of doors, screens and wall panelling, hand carved

T J Harwood & Co Ltd
Ellenshaw Works, Kay St, Darwen, Lancashire BB3 3EW
Telephone: 0254 775225
Specialities: porcelain door furniture, doorplates and knobs

Havenplan's Architectural Emporium
The Old Station, Station Rd, Killamarsh, Nr Sheffield, South Yorkshire S31 8EN
Telephone: 0742 489972
Specialities: oak, pine and mahogany doors

Knobs and Knockers
36–40 York Way, London N1 9AB
Telephone: 01 278 8925
50 shops nationwide

B Lilly & Sons Ltd
Baltimore Rd, Birmingham B42 1DJ
Telephone: 021 357 1761
Specialities: solid brass handles and fittings from authentic patterns dating back to 1861

Lionheart Decorative Hardware (Hope Works) Ltd

Pleck Rd, Walsall, West Midlands WS2 9HH
Telephone: 0922 27175

Locks and Handles of South Kensington
8 Exhibition Rd, South Kensington, London SW7 2HF
Telephone: 01 584 6800

The London Door Co
165 St Johns Hill, London SW11 1TQ
Telephone: 01 223 7243
Specialities: internal and external doors, some original, others made to order, decorative glass panels, sandblasted, etched and stained

M & A Main
The Old Smithy, Cerrig-Y-Drudion, Nr Corwen, North Wales LL21 9SR
Telephone: 049 082 491

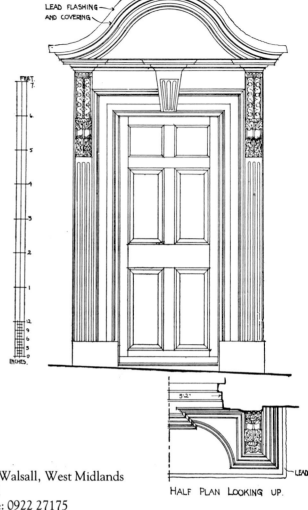

LEAD FLASHING AND COVERING

HALF PLAN LOOKING UP.

Nº 12 BARNHILL
STAMFORD LINCS

Specialities: reclaimed panelling, newels, spindles, handrails, architraves, pews, mouldings, reclaimed timber, six and four panel doors, brassware, cast iron balusters, balconies, railings, kitchen ranges, cast iron fireplaces

Marcus Ltd (Heritage Brass)
Embassy Works, Attwood St, Lye,
Nr Stourbridge, West Midlands
DY9 8RY
Telephone: 0384 892461

Josiah Parkes & Sons Ltd
Union Works, Gower St,
Willenhall, West Midlands
WV13 1JX
Telephone: 0902 366931
Specialities: locks

Rothley Brass Ltd and Albion Hardware Ltd
71 Allesley St, Birmingham
B6 4ND
Telephone: 021 359 8911

A Touch of Brass
61 Fulham High St, London SW6
Telephone: 01 731 6100
Specialities: quality brassware—
door knobs, knockers, letter
plates, china door furniture

Yannedis & Co Ltd
25–27 Theobalds Rd, London
WC1X 8SR
Telephone: 01 242 7106
Specialities: architectural
ironmongers, reproduction door
furniture

Yorkshire Stripping Service
Mill Farm, Kirk Hammerton, Nr
Green Hammerton, York
Telephone: 0901 30451
Restoration: pine furniture
Specialities: pine doors and
furniture, architectural artifacts,
courier service, collection and
delivery arranged, shipping,
export and retail

FIREPLACES AND ACCESSORIES

Robert Aagaard
Frogmire House, Stockwell Rd,
Knaresborough, North Yorkshire
HG5 0JP
Telephone: 0423 864805

Acres Farm Fenders
Bradfield, Berkshire RG7 6J8
Telephone: 0734 744305

Specialities: brass fenders, brass
and leather seated club fenders
by mail order only

Amazing Grates
Phoenix House, 61–63 High Rd,
East Finchley, London N2 8AB
Telephone: 01 883 9590
Specialities: Reproduction tiled
and arched insert grates, pine
and mahogany mantels. Original
Georgian and Victorial marble
mantels

Aquisitions (Fireplaces) Ltd
269 Camden High St, London
NW1 7BX
Telephone: 01 485 4955
Specialities: Reproduction
Victorian/Edwardian fireplaces
and accessories

Ashburton Marbles
6 West St, Ashburton, Devon
Telephone: 0364 53189
Specialities: marble fire surrounds

Bailey's Architectural Antiques
The Engine Shed, Ashburton
Industrial Estate, Ross-on-Wye,
Herefordshire HR9 7BW
Telephone: 0989 63015
Specialities: period fireplaces,
stained glass, bathroom fittings,
decorative ironwork

Barry Restorations
2a Jewel St, Barry, Glamorgan,
South Wales CF6 6NQ
Telephone: 0446 744788
Specialities: original fireplaces and
surrounds

Nigel Bartlett
67 St Thomas St, London SE1
Telephone: 01 378 7895
Specialities: antique
chimneypieces in marble, stone
and wood

Britannia Ltd
5 Normandy St, Alton, Hampshire
GU34 1DD

Telephone: 0420 84427
Specialities: replica iron fire grates

T F Buckle (London) Ltd
427 Kings Rd, London SW10 0LR
Telephone: 01 352 0952
Specialities: fine antique pine and
marble fireplaces

Burley Appliances Ltd
Pillings Rd, Oakham, Rutland,
Leicestershire LE15 6QF
Telephone: 0572 56956
Specialities: log-effect electric fires,
hand-forged fire baskets with
solid brass decoration, free-
standing or inset

Camden Antiques
35a Upper Camden St, North
Shields, Tyne & Wear
Telephone: 0632 581027
Specialities: antique fireplaces

**Capricorn Architectural Ironwork
Ltd**

Tasso Forge, Tasso Yard, 56 Tasso
Rd, London W6 8LZ
Telephone: 01 381 4235
Specialities: firebacks, dogs and
grates

The Cast Iron Fireplace Co Ltd
99–103 East Hill, Wandsworth,
London SW18 2QB
Telephone: 01 870 1630
Specialities: fireplaces from 1830 to
present day

Chapel House Fireplaces
Netherfield House, St George's Rd,
Scholes, Holmfirth, Huddersfield,
W Yorks HD7 1UH
Telephone: 0484 682275
Specialities: antique and Victorian
fireplaces and mantelpieces.
Telephone for an appointment

Chimneypieces
227 Westbourne Grove, London
W11
Telephone: 01 727 0102
Specialities: period fireplaces in
marble, cast iron and old pine.
Large selection of grates

Chowne & Francis Ltd
No 1 Hanger, Ford Airfield, Nr
Arundel, Sussex BN18 0BN
Telephone: 0903 723541
Specialities: hand-carved pine and
mahogany fireplaces, period and
modern

Classic Surroundings Ltd
171 Fortess Rd, Kentish Town,
London NW5
Telephone: 01 267 9084/ 485 2445/
267 1909

W H Collier Ltd
Church Lane, Marks Tey,
Colchester, Essex CO6 1LN
Telephone: 0206 210301
Specialities: handmade fireplace
briquettes

Crowthers of Syon Lodge
Bush Corner, London Rd,
Isleworth, Middlesex TW7 5BH
Telephone: 01 560 7978
Specialities: Fine antique fireplaces

J Day (Stoneworks)
Church Lane, Colney Heath, St

Albans, Herts AR4 0NH
Telephone: 0727 23326
Specialities: cast iron and wooden surrounds, marble, stonework and tile inserts, fireplace accessories

Fireplace Design Ltd
157c Great Portland St, London W1N 5FB
Telephone: 01 580 9893
Specialities: fireplaces, grates

Robin Gage
Unit 7, The Talina Centre, Bagley's Lane, London SW6 2BW
Telephone: 01 731 1370
Specialities: club fenders

Glover & Stacey
Malthouse Premises, Main Rd, Kingsley, Nr Bordon, Hampshire
Telephone: 04203 5754
Specialities: antique fireplaces

Glynwed Consumer & Building Products Ltd
Ketley, Telford, Shropshire TF1 3BR
Telephone: 0952 641414

Grate Restorations
27 Western Rd, Hove, Sussex BN3 1AF
Telephone: 0273 737784
Specialities: original and reproduction fireplaces

Hallidays Antiques Ltd
The Old College, Dorchester-on-Thames, Oxfordshire OX9 8HL
Telephone: 0865 340028/68
Telex: 83147 'Pine'
London showrooms:
28 Beauchamp Place, Knightsbridge, London SW3 1NJ
Telephone: 01 589 5534
Specialities: reproduction eighteenth- and nineteenth-century carved pine mantelpieces

Havenplan's Architectural Emporium
The Old Station, Killamarsh, Nr Sheffield, South Yorkshire S31 8EN
Telephone: 0742 489972
Specialities: cast iron Victorian

fireplaces, doors in oak, pine and mahogany plus wrought iron gates

Hodkin & Jones (Sheffield) Ltd
Dunston House, Dunston Rd, Sheep Bridge, Chesterfield, Derbyshire S41 9QD
Telephone: 0246 455255
Specialities: plaster fire surrounds

Hollingshead & Co
783 Fulham Rd, London SW6
Telephone: 01 863 6886/ 736 6991
Specialities: marble and pine, antique and reproduction mantelpieces

Philip Hough Ltd
High St, Norley, Nr Frodsham, Cheshire WA6 8JZ
Telephone: 0928 88692
Specialities: inglenook fireplaces and other accessories

House of Steel
400 Caledonian Rd, London N1 1DA
Telephone: 01 607 5889
Specialities: large selection of Victorian and Edwardian cast

iron fireplaces, statues and garden furniture, beds, staircases, metalwork, stonework, furniture

Interoven Ltd
Fearnley House, 70–72 Fearnley St, Watford, Hertfordshire WD1 7DE
Telephone: 0923 46761
Specialities: traditional firebacks and grates, welded steel solid fuel stoves

George Jackson & Sons Ltd
Rathbone Works, Rainville Rd, London W6 9HD
Telephone: 01 385 6616/7/8
Specialities: architectural ornaments and fireplaces

Kingsworthy Foundry Co Ltd
London Rd, Kingsworthy, Winchester, Hampshire SO23 7QG
Telephone: 0962 883776
Specialities: everything for the fireplace, garden furniture

Knight's of London
2A Belsize Park Mews, Belsize

Village, London NW3 5BL
Telephone: 01 431 2490
Specialities: antique and period fireplaces

M & A Main
The Old Smithy, Cerrig-Y-Drudion, Nr Corwen, North Wales LL21 9SR
Telephone: 049 082 491
Specialities: cast iron fireplaces, pubs, panelling, leaded glass

Marble Hill Fireplaces Ltd
72 Richmond Rd, Twickenham, Middlesex TW1 3BE
Telephone: 01 892 1488/8460
Specialities: antique marble and hand carved pine fireplaces

Morpeth Craft Joinery
Unit 3D, Coopies Field, Coopies Lane Industrial Estate, Morpeth, Northumberland NE61 6JT
Telephone: 0670 511159
Specialities: period fireplaces in pine, dressers

Nostalgia Architectural Antiques
61B Shaw Heath, Stockport, Cheshire FK3 8BH
Telephone: 061 477 7706
Specialities: fully restored antique fireplaces in marble, cast iron, mahogany, oak, pine and stone

Old World Trading Co
565 Kings Rd, London SW6 2EB
Telephone: 01 731 4708
Specialities: eighteenth- and nineteenth-century marble, wood and stone fireplaces

The Original Choice
1340 Stratford Rd, Hall Green, Birmingham B28 9EH
Telephone: 021 778 3821
Specialities: original and reproduction fireplaces in pine, marble, mahogany, oak and cast iron, all types of fireplace accessory, stained glass

Oxford Architectural Trading
27 Cowley Rd, Oxford OX4 1HP
Telephone: 0865 249666

Pageant Antiques
122 Dawes Rd, London SW6

117

DETAIL OF CORNICE TO PIERS

Centre Line of Piers

Round

Telephone: 01 385 7739
Specialities: antique fireplaces

Pages Shopping Centre
1–3 Brockenhurst Rd, South
Ascot, Berkshire SL5 9DJ
Telephone: 0990 24714
Telex: 847401
Fax: 0990 23118
Specialities: Adam style fireplaces,
marble

Patrick Fireplaces
Guildford Rd, Farnham, Surrey
GU9 9QA
Telephone: 0252 722345
Specialities: individually designed
marble, slate and stone fireplaces

Petit Roque Ltd
5a New Rd, Croxley Green,
Rickmansworth, Hertfordshire
WD3 3EJ
Telephone: 0923 779291
Specialities: polished marble
fireplace suites, hearths, back
panels, stone and wooden
mantel surrounds and shelves

G R Phipps & Co
Cumnor Hill, Oxford OX2 9PH
Telephone: 0865 863363
Specialities: carved pine
mantelpieces

Phoenix Fireplaces Ltd
51 Lark Lane, Liverpool,
Merseyside L17 8UW
Telephone: 051 727 3578

The Pine Place
59 St Leonards Rd, Windsor, Berks
SL4 3BX
Telephone: 0753 862926

Poyner & Weatherley
Stoneyard, Dorset Rd, London
N15
Telephone: 01 800 4559
Specialities: cleaning of marble fire
surrounds, also made to order

Puritan Forge Ltd
PO Box 287, London SE23 3TN
Telephone: 01 669 8281
Specialities: fire doors and curtains

Quality Stonework
Cowfold Rd, West Grinstead,

Horsham, Sussex RH13 3DF
Telephone: 0403 864232

Rainford House of Elegance
Wentworth St, Birdwell, Barnsley,
West Yorkshire S70 5UN
Telephone: 0226 745129
Specialities: period fire surrounds
   and architectural mouldings,
   marble hearths, brass fenders

Real Flame
80 New King's Rd, London
SW6 4LT
Telephone: 01 731 2704
Specialities: log and gas coal fires

Renaissance Period Fireplaces
Norwood Industrial Estate,
Killamarsh, Sheffield S31 8HB
Telephone: 0742 488025
Specialities: replica fireplaces

Simplicity Fires
The Bishop Centre, Bath Rd,
Taplow, Maidenhead, Bucks
SL6 0NX
Specialities: gas/log effect fires,
   marble and stone, cast iron
   Victorian surrounds

James Smellie Ltd
Stafford St, Dudley, West
Midlands DY1 2AD
Telephone: 0384 52320
Specialities: period fire grates and
   backs

Stylecast
Unit 17, Laurence Industrial
Estate, Eastwardbury Lane,
Southend-on-Sea
Telephone: 0702 520181
Specialities: historic mantelpieces

Turret Antiques
565 George St, Aberdeen,
Scotland AB2 3XX
Telephone: 0224 635404
Specialities: marble fireplaces,
   antique carved chimneypieces

Verdigris
Unit B18, Clerkenwell Workshops,
31 Clerkenwell Close, London EC1
Telephone: 01 253 7788
Specialities: metalwork restoration

Vermont Castings Inc.

2nd Floor, 44 Friar Gate, Derby
DE1 1DA
Telephone: 0332 372 199
Specialities: woodburning stoves

S F Walker
Stone & Marblemason,
24 Fiddlebridge Industrial Centre,
Lemsford Rd, Hatfield,
Hertfordshire
Telephone: 07072 68857

Mr Wandle's Workshop
200–202 Garratt Lane, London
SW18 4ED
Telephone: 01 870 5873
Specialities: Victorian and
   Edwardian fireplace specialists

Whitchurch
5 York Parade, Great West Rd,
Brentford, Essex
Telephone: 01 560 0927
Specialities: stone fireplaces,
   period surrounds, marble,
   Continental fireplaces

Wonderfire
1/7 Smyth Rd, Bedminster, Bristol
Telephone: 0272 637071

GARDEN SOURCES

Allibert Ltd
Berry Hill Industrial Estate,
Droitwich, Worcestershire
WR9 9AB
Telephone: 0905 774221
Specialities: garden furniture

Almondsbury Forge
Sundays Hill, Almondsbury,
Bristol BS2 4DS
Telephone: 0454 613315
Specialities: weathervanes, gates,
   railings, restoration of old gates

David Arbus
The Granary, Railway Hill,
Barham, Nr Canterbury, Kent
Telephone: 0227 831540
Specialities: Rattan furniture

Barlow Tyrie Ltd
Springwood Industrial Estate,
Braintree, Essex CM7 7RN
Telephone: 0376 22505

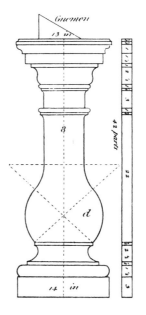

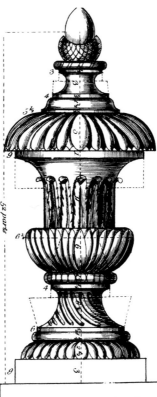

The Profiles are figured from the
centeral lines of the Vase.

Beacon Garden Centres Ltd
Stubbings House, Henley Rd,
Maidenhead, Berkshire SL6 6QL
Telephone: 0628 825454
Specialities: garden furniture

Bewdley Brass Foundry
Bewdley Museum, Load St,

Bewdley, Worcestershire
DY12 2AE
Telephone: 0299 403575
Specialities: brass sundials

Brambley Garden Furniture
4 Crittall Drive, Springwood
Industrial Estate, Braintree, Essex
CM7 7QX
Telephone: 0376 20210
Specialities: garden furniture

**Capricorn Architectural Ironwork
Ltd**
Tasso Forge, Tasso Yard, 56 Tasso
Rd, London W6 8LZ
Telephone: 01 381 4235
Specialities: weathervanes

Chilstone Garden Ornaments
Sprivers Estate, Horsmonden, Kent
TN12 8DR
Telephone: 089 272 3553
Specialities: architectural and
   garden ornaments, fountains,
   statues, urns, temples,
   balustrading, columns, coping,
   bench seats and sundials

Classic Furniture (Newport) Ltd
Audley Avenue, Newport,
Shropshire TF10 7DE
Telephone: 0952 813311
Specialities: cast iron garden
   furniture, spiral staircases, dog
   grates, stoves

Clifton Nurseries Ltd
Clifton Villas, Warwick Avenue,
London W9 2PH
Telephone: 01 289 6851

Andrew Crace Designs
Bourne Lane, Much Hadham,
Hertfordshire SG10 6ER
Telephone: 0279 84 2685
Specialities: classic garden
   furniture in the best tradition of
   the English country house

Mike Deasy Ltd
108–114 Eastern Rd, Brighton,
Sussex BN2 2AJ
Telephone: 0273 688523
Specialities: marble and cement
   figures, urns, seats, tables,
   columns, well heads and
   fountains

Forecast Furniture
34 Avenue Rd, London NW8 6BU
Telephone: 01 722 8698
Specialities: garden furniture

Forsham Cottage Arts
Goreside Farm, Great Chart,
Ashford, Kent TN26 1JU
Telephone: 023382 229

Garden Crafts
158 New Kings Rd, Fulham,
London SW6 4LZ
Telephone: 01 736 1615
Specialities: garden ornaments and
traditional garden furniture

Gloster Leisure Furniture Ltd
Universal House, Pennywell Rd,
Bristol BS5 OTJ
Telephone: 0272 540349
Specialities: garden furniture

Green Brothers (GEEBRO) Ltd
South Rd, Hailsham, East Sussex
BN27 3DE
Telephone: 0323 840771
Specialities: garden furniture

House of Steel
400 Caledonian Rd, London
N1 1DN
Telephone: 01 607 5889
Specialities: large selection of
metal garden furniture, statues,
stonework

Jardine Leisure Furniture Ltd
Rosemount Towers, Wallington
Square, Wallington, Surrey
SM6 8RR
Telephone: 01 669 8265
Specialities: garden furniture

Kentish Ironcraft Ltd
Ashford Rd, Bethersden, Ashford,
Kent TN26 3AT
Telephone: 0233 82465
Specialities: weathervanes

King Easton Ltd
The Green, Station Rd,
Winchmore Hill, London
N21 3NB
Telephone: 01 886 8783

Kingsworthy Foundry Co Ltd
London Rd, Kingsworthy,
Winchester, Hampshire

SO23 7QG
Telephone: 0962 883776
Specialities: garden furniture

Leisure Plan Sales
28 Windhill, Bishops Stortford,
Hertfordshire CM23 2NG
Telephone: 0279 505525

Peter Leth's Workbench
Farland Rillaton, Rilla Mill,
Callington, Cornwall PL7 7PA
Telephone: 0579 62388
Specialities: weathervanes

B Levy & Co (Patterns) Ltd
37 Churton St, Westminster,
London SW1
Telephone: 01 834 7846
Specialities: weathervanes

Minsterstone Garden Ornaments
Station Rd, Ilminster, Somerset
TA19 9AS
Telephone: 04605 2277
Specialities: Portland, Doulting
and Ham Hill stone garden
ornaments, balustrading

Nova Garden Furniture
Graveney Rd, Faversham, Kent
ME13 8UN
Telephone: 0795 535511
Specialities: garden furniture

Ollerton Engineering
Samlesbury Mills, Goosefoot Lane,
Samlesbury Bottoms, Preston,
Lancashire PR5 ORN
Telephone: 025 485 2127
Specialities: gazebos and rose
arches in galvanized steel

Richard Quinnell Ltd
Rowhurst Forge, Oxshott Rd,
Leatherhead, Surrey KT22 OEN
Telephone: 0372 375 148
Specialities: weathervanes

Reece Originals
The Chippings, Wrights Lane,
Sutton Bridge, Lincolnshire
PE12 9RH
Telephone: 0406 350989
Specialities: African Iroko hard
wood and weather treated
wrought iron

Renaissance Casting

102 Arnold Avenue, Styvechale,
Coventry CV3 5NE
Telephone: 0203 27275
Specialities: fountains and garden
furnishings

Rokes Ltd
Woodside Works, Andoversford,
Cheltenham, Gloucestershire
GL54 5RJ
Telephone: 04515 413
Specialities: statues, Regency style
planters, balustrading, bird baths
and sundials in local Cotswold
stone

Rose du Temps Passe
Woodlands House, Stretton, Nr
Stafford, Staffordshire ST19 9LG
Telephone: 0785 840217

Secret Gardens
171 Pinner Rd, Watford Heath,
Oxhey, Hertfordshire WD1 4EP

Telephone: 0923 51975
Specialities: garden design service

Shedlow Ltd
Badlingham Rd, Framlingham, Nr
Woodbridge, Suffolk IP13 9HS
Telephone: 0728 724044/723041
Specialities: Victorian styled
garden furniture, urns, gazebos

Solstice
Unit E2, Colchester Factory Estate,
Colchester Avenue, Cardiff
CF3 7AP
Telephone: 0222 488205
Specialities: sundials made in solid
brass and Welsh slate

Tiger Developments Ltd
Deanland Rd, Golden Cross, Nr
Hailsham, East Sussex
Telephone: 0825 872555
Specialities: bridges, lakes and
gazebos for gardens and estates

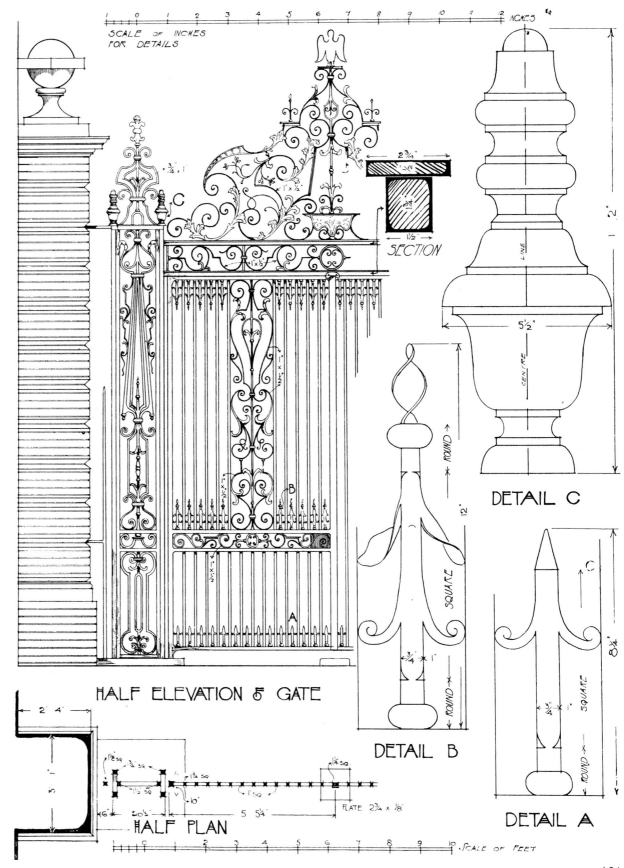

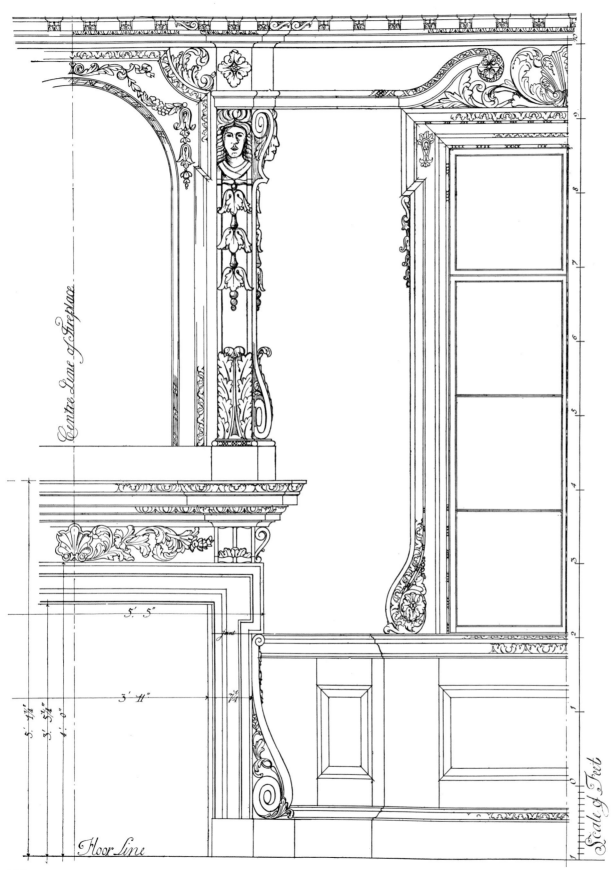

Centre Line of Fireplace

Floor Line

Scale of Feet

5' 5"

3' 11"

7½"

5' 1¼"
5' 5¼"
4' 0"

Joint

S9 2LR
Telephone: 0742 561156

W Birch & Sons
Foss Allen Rd, York YO3 7UP
Telephone: 0904 22185

Cement and Plaster Mouldings Ltd
Brittania Rd, Ipswich, Suffolk
IP4 4PE
Telephone: 0473 73421
Specialities: pargetting and
  decorative plasterwork. Projects
  include work on the Ancient
  House, Ipswich

Christos Interiors Ltd
85a Church Rd, Hendon, London
NW4
Telephone: 01 203 5940/5450
Specialities: cornices, internal
  arches and columns, panel
  moulds, fire surrounds, GRP
  columns and porticoes

Clark & Fen Ltd
Mitcham House, 681 Mitcham Rd,
Croydon, Surrey CR9 3AP
Telephone: 01 689 2266

Classical Designs
1387 London Rd, Leigh-on-Sea,
Essex
Telephone: 0702 78392/714177
Specialities: architectural
  ornaments

CMH Mouldings
6–8 John St, Porthcawl, Mid-
Glamorgan
Telephone: 065671 8283
Specialities: niches, cornices, door
  surrounds, fire surrounds, arches,
  corbels, centrepieces, plaques
  and columns

Copley Decor Mouldings
Bedale Rd, Leyburn, North
Yorkshire DL8 5QA
Telephone: 0969 23410
US Office:
Royal American Wallcraft Inc,
Crown House, 834 South West
Side 1, Fort Pierce, Florida
FL33450 USA
Specialities: decor mouldings but
  not with traditional materials

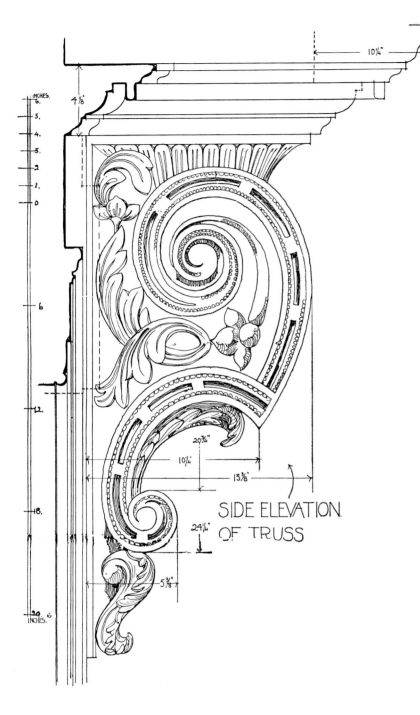

SIDE ELEVATION.
OF TRUSS

W G Crotch & Sons
119 Fore St, Ipswich, Suffolk
IP4 1LF
Telephone: 0473 50349
Restoration: period and modern
moulds dating from 1700 AD.
Specialist decorating, gilding,
rag rolling and marbling

**Designed Plastercraft Associates
Ltd**

244–254 Cambridge Heath Rd,
London E2
Telephone: 01 981 7427
Specialities: fibrous plaster

Design Interiors
Unit 3, Peartree Business Centre,
Peartree Rd, Stanway, Colchester,
Essex
Telephone: 0206 563421
Specialities handcrafted plaster

mouldings, arches, niches,
cornices, wall and ceiling panels,
fire surrounds, dado rails

Hayles & Howe
Picton House, 25 Picton St,
Montpelier, Bristol BS6 5PZ
Telephone: 0272 46673

Hodkin & Jones Ltd
23 Rathbone Place, London
W1P 1DV
Telephone: 01 636 2617
Specialities: fibrous plaster
mouldings

G Jackson & Sons
Rathbone Works, Rainville Rd,
London W6 9HD
Telephone: 01 385 6616
Specialities: fibrous and solid
plastering, period and modern

London Fine Art Plaster Ltd
444 Hackney Rd, Treadway St,
London E2 6QW
Telephone: 01 739 3594
Specialities: architectural and
decorative fibrous plasterers

J G McDonough Ltd
347 New Kings Rd, London
SW6 4RJ
Telephone: 01 736 5146

E G Millar (Plastering) Ltd
54 Hawkwood Crescent,
Chingford, London E4 7PJ
Telephone: 01 529 0431

Pages Shopping Centre
1–3 Brockenhurst Rd, South
Ascot, Berkshire SL5 9DJ
Telephone: 0990 24714
Specialities: cornices, panel
mouldings, columns, arches,
niches and corbels

Paxdale Castings Ltd
3 Ajax Works, Hertford Rd,
Barking, Essex IG11 8BN
Telephone: 01 591 0434
Specialities: decorative and
ornamental plasterwork,
columns, cornices, niches,
arches, panel moulding

**PCC International (Marble &
Tiles) Ltd/Period Mouldings Ltd**

20–24 Commercial Rd, Gloucester
GL1 2EG
Telephone: 0452 418742
Specialities: fibrous plaster
mouldings — ceiling centres,
dado rails, arches, niches,
columns

The Plaster Decoration Co Ltd
30 Stannary St, London SE11 4AE
Telephone: 01 735 8161

Jane Schofield
Stephens', Shepton Beauchamp,
Ilminster, Somerset TA19 0RB
Telephone: 0460 41033
Restoration: re-hanging, repair,
cleaning and conservation of
ornamental plasterwork from
sixteenth to eighteenth centuries

L Stead & Son
Victoria Fibrous Plasterworks,
Eccleshill, Bradford, West
Yorkshire BD2 2DJ
Telephone: 0274 37222

T & O Plaster Castings
7 Collier Row Rd, Collier Rd,
Romford, Essex RM5 3NT
Telephone: 0708 45619

Thomas & Wilson Ltd
454 Fulham Rd, London SW6 1BA
Telephone: 01 381 1161/7
Specialities: architectural
ornaments

Traditional Interiors
16–18 Lower Kings Rd,
Berkhamstead, Hertfordshire
HP4 2AE
Telephone: 044 27 5501
Specialities: fire surrounds, niches,
corniches, archways

Veronese Ltd
Interiors House, Lynton Rd,
Crouch End, London N8 8AE
Telephone: 01 348 9262

RESTORATION

David Ackroyd
Bleathwood Manor Farm,
Bleathwood, Ludlow, Shropshire
SY8 4LT
Telephone: 0584 810726

Specialities: all types of high quality woodwork restoration drawing on extensive stocks of mature rare woods and timbers. Projects include work on Woburn Abbey and several National Trust properties

Dorothea Restoration Engineers Ltd
Pearl Assurance House, Hardwick St, Buxton, Derbyshire SK17 6DH
Telephone: 0298 3834
Specialities: traditional and modern design, manufacture and restoration of railings, gates in cast and fabricated metalwork

Eaton-Gaze Ltd
86 Teesdale St, London E2 6PU
Telephone: 01 739 7272/3
Showrooms: 22 The Broadway, The Bourne, Southgate, London N14

Hagen Restorations
Bakehouse Cottage, Northwood End, Haynes, Bedfordshire MK45 3QD
Telephone: 023066 424
Specialities: conservation and restoration of panelled doors and non-structural woodwork including painted wooden surfaces. Specialist woodworm

treatment for antique woodwork

John Henderson Ltd
Inglis Lane, Castleblair, Dunfermline, Fife KY12 9DP
Telephone: 0383 721123/723714
Specialities: restoration of wrought iron, mild steel, cast iron balcony rails, gates, railing, arches, fabrication in traditional designs with new materials

Heritage Tile Conservation
C14 Maws Craft Centre, Jackfield, Telford, Shropshire TF8 7LS
Telephone: 0952 883961
Specialities: removal and

restoration of ceramic architectural detailing including pictorial tiled panels, ceramic friezes, fountains and façades. Projects have included work on Harrods Food Hall—the cleaning and restoration of the tiled hunting frieze

J S R Joinery
Pool St, Great Yeldham, Halstead, Essex CO9 4HN
Telephone: 0787 237722
Specialities: exact copies of existing old windows, doors, staircases

V A Manners & Son
313 Hurst Rd, Bexley, Kent
DA5 3DZ
Telephone: 01 300 9356
Specialities: restoration of fine
antique woodwork including
panelling, doors, bookcases,
staircases. Projects include work
on the Maritime Museum at
Greenwich

Hector B Moore
The Forge, Brandeston,
Woodbridge, Suffolk IP13 7AN
Telephone: 072 882 354
Specialities: manufacture and
restoration of decorative,
architectural and ecclesiastical
metalwork. Patternwork and
decorative castings supplied to
suit client's designs

Andrew Naylor
Unit H3, Halesfield 19, Telford,
Shropshire TF7 4QT
Telephone: 0952 583116
Specialities: conservation and
restoration of all types of metal
sculpture and ornament

Optimum Brasses
7 Castle Street, Bampton,
Tiverton, Devon EX16 9NS
Telephone: 0398 31515
Specialities: the very best brassware
for antique restoration

John Sambrook
Park House, Northam, East Sussex
TN31 6PA
Telephone: 07974 2615
Specialities: fanlight making.
Projects include work on
property in Grafton Way,
London making two copies of an
existing fanlight for a new
shopfront

D J Smith
34 Silchester Rd, Pamber Heath,
Nr Basingstoke, Hampshire
RG26 6EF
Telephone: 0734 700595
Specialities: restoration and gilding
of woodwork of all periods with a
speciality for eighteenth-century
woodcarvings—fine carved
mirrors, torchers, figures and
animal sculpture

Margaret Spencer
Chard Rd, Crewkerne, Somerset
TA18 8BA
Telephone: 0460 72362
Specialities: Rocking horse maker
and restorer, also fairground
horses

Thomas & Wilson
454 Fulham Rd, London SW6 1BY
Telephone: 01 381 1161
Specialities: restoration and
reproduction of decorative
plasterwork

M P Wallis
Norfolk Cottage, 1 The Row,
Hawridge Common, Nr Chesham,
Bucks HP5 2UH
Telephone: 024 029 8172
Specialities: metal polishing, wood
turning, glasswork, boule,
gilding

D W Windsor Ltd
Pindar Rd, Hoddesdon, Herts
EN11 0EZ
Telephone: 0992 445666
Telex: 263311 Winsor G
Specialities: restoration of
Victorian copper lanterns and
Victorian cast iron lamp posts.
Projects include renovation of
original Victorian globe lanterns
at the Royal Military Academy,
Sandhurst, and renovation of
nineteenth-century lamps from
the perimeter wall of Trafalgar
Square

SALVAGE AUCTIONS

Brillscote Farm Auctions
Brillscote Farm, Lea, Malmesbury,
Wiltshire
Telephone: 0666 822332
London Office: 127 St Pancras Rd,
London NW1
Telephone: 01388 2691/01 387
6039
Specialities: architectural auctions,
regular sales of architectural
fixtures and fittings, fairground
art, shop fittings, stained and
etched glass, garden ornaments
and gazebos, summerhouses,
transport items, hand carts,

perambulators for young and old,
early aeroplane propellors,
enamelled signs, inn signs,
banners

Dennis Pocock
20 High Street, Marlborough
SN8 1AA
Telephone: 0672 53471/2
Specialities: infrequent sales of
antique building materials

Posterity Architectural Effects
Baldwin's Farm, Newent, Gloucs
GL18 1LS
Telephone: 053 185 597
Specialities: ironwork balcony
fronts and columns, sporting
fittings and memorabilia,
sections of old grandstands, cast
iron conservatory fittings, garden
furniture, bathroom fittings,
doors, windows, fireplace
surrounds. Biannual auction
sales in April and October

STAINED GLASS

Allant Design
Springwood Cottage, Springwood
Rd, Rawdon, Leeds LS19 6BH
Telephone: 0532 577474
(0532 505676 evenings)

**The Birmingham Glass Art Co
Ltd**
18c Vyse Street, Hockley,
Birmingham B18 6LE
Telephone: 021 523 4789
Specialities: Lead, Tiffany copper
foil, glass slumping (bending),
painting, transfer application
and silk screening

BSD Stained Glass
40 Acton Lane, Chiswick, London
W4 5ED
Telephone: 01 994 3212
Specialities: doors, windows,
vertical panels, Tiffany panels

Crystal Lines
Unit 66, Fox's Factory, Tonedale
Mill, Wellington, Somerset
TA21 0AW
Telephone: 0823 47 6671

Specialities: Stained glass windows
and panels

Dragonfly Glass
Unit 97/3E
Park View Industrial Estate, Brenda
Rd, Hartlepool, Cleveland
TS25 1PG
Telephone: 0429 77617
Specialities: Stained glass shades in
Tiffany, Art Deco and Victorian
styles, panels, doors, windows

Glass Galleries
PO Box 112, Enfield, Middlesex
Telephone: 01 363 1353
Specialities: doors, windows,
Tiffany lampshades
Restoration: restorations and
architectural work undertaken

Glass Restoration
137 Queen's Crescent, Kentish
Town, London NW5 4EG
Telephone: 01 482 2272
Restoration: all types of restoration
work undertaken, re-glazing in
plain or leaded lights

Glasslight Studios Ltd
The Old Pumphouse, Gloucester
Place, The Maritime Quarter,
Swansea SA1 1TY
Telephone: 0792 472595

Goddard & Gibbs Studios Ltd
41–49 Kingsland Rd, London
E2 8AD
Telephone: 01 739 6563
Telex: 297701 Stglas G
Restoration: Repair and
restoration of all forms of stained
glass, leaded lights and
'Copperlights'
Specialities: Designers and
manufacturers of bespoke
decorative and stained glass,
leaded lights and 'Copperlight'
fire-retardant glazing. Clients
include Tower Bridge, London,
the Royal Naval College,
Greenwich, the Royal Hospital,
Chelsea and stained glass repairs
at the Palace of Westminster

**Dennis Hollingsworth
M.S.M.G.P.**
Omega Stained Glass Studio,
Campion Drive, Swinton,

Mexborough, South Yorkshire
S64 8QZ
Telephone: 0709 587034
Restoration: Yes
Specialities: Manufacture and restoration of stained glass and leaded lights, ecclesiastical, commercial and domestic. The studio specialises in the design and production of kiln-fired stained glass roundels to set into doors or, more usually today, hand in windows. These roundels were originally produced in the fifteenth and sixteenth centuries to commemorate special events and anniversaries and this traditional use for stained glass is being revived—usually with naturalistic birds, animals and flowers.

Matthew Lloyd Stained Glass Studio
63 Amberley Rd, Palmers Green, London N13 4BH
Telephone: 01 886 0213
Restoration: Matthew Lloyd has had eight years' experience in stained glass fabrication and restoration of Victorian and later glass.
Specialities: Design, fabrication and restoration of leaded glass mainly for home and domestic work. Clients are welcome to visit the studio by appointment to discuss individual commissions.

The London Door Co
165 St Johns Hill, London
SW11 1TQ
Telephone: 01 223 7243

Specialities: Decorative glass panels, sandblasted, etched and stained.

M & A Main
The Old Smithy, Cerrig-Y-Drudion, Nr Corwen, North Wales LL21 9SR
Telephone: 049 082 491
Specialities: Reclaimed Victorian stained glass

Andrew Moor Associates
131 High Holborn, London
WC1 6PS
Telephone: 01 242 9902
Specialities: Contemporary stained glass commissions

MS Glass Decorators
51 Enterprise Drive, Streetley, Sutton Coldfield B74 2DY
Telephone: 021 352 0432
Specialities: Etched decorative windows, door screens and mirrors

Michael O'Connor
2 Belgrave Place, Southport, Merseyside
Telephone: 0704 65681

The Original Choice
1340 Stratford Rd, Hall Green, Birmingham B28 9EH
Telephone: 021 778 3821
Restoration: Yes
Specialities: Antique stained glass doors and windows, repair and commissions undertaken

James Preece
11 Portobello Green, 281 Portobello Rd, London W10 5TD

Telephone: 01 968 8807
Specialities: Windows, doors, screens, skylights, conservatories, lamps

John Sambrook
Park House, Northiam, East Sussex TN31 6PA
Telephone: 07974 2615
Specialities: Hand-built fanlights

R A Smith
49 Smith House Crescent, Brighouse, West Yorkshire HD6 2LB
Telephone: 0484 720781
Specialities: Modern or traditional stained glass commissions
Restoration: Skilful repair and restoration service to existing stained glass

Anne Sotheran
6 St Peter's Grove, Bootham, York
Telephone: 0904 641066
Specialities: commissions in stained glass, examples of which can be seen in the Visitors' Centre at Coventry Cathedral

Stained Glass Overlay UK Ltd
PO Box 65, Anson Rd, Norwich NR6 6EJ
Telephone: 0603 485454
Telex: 975047
Specialities: An American system for converting plain glass to the coloured variety in situ. Operated on a franchise system with local craftsmen

Townsends Architectural Antiques
36 New End Square, Hampstead, London NW3 1LF

Telephone: 01 794 5706/7
Specialities: Design and fabrication of stained glass windows

Victorian Stained Glass Co
83 Stamford Hill, London N16 5TP
Telephone: 01 800 9008

Whiteway & Waldron Ltd
305 Munster Rd, London SW6
Telephone: 01 381 3195
Restoration: Yes
Specialities: Sales and repair

THATCH

Cosy Thatch Ltd
The Oaks, Myddlewood, Nr Shrewsbury, Shropshire
Telephone: 0939 260449
Specialities: roof thatchers, Norfolk Reed and Wheat Reed, thatched porches, wishing wells, thatched umbrellas and summer houses

National Society of Master Thatchers
73 Hughenden Ave, Downley, High Wycombe, Buckinghamshire
Telephone: 0494 443198

J D Raison & Partners
1 Deer Park Court, Stratford-upon-Avon, Staffordshire CV37 OPQ
Telephone: 0789 295236
Specialities: thatched porches

Thatching Advisory Service Ltd
Rose Tree Farm, 29 Nine Mile Ride, Finchampstead, Wokingham, Berkshire RG11 4QD
Telephone: 0734 734203

US SOURCES

ARCHITECTURAL SALVAGE

The Architectural Antique Warehouse
PO Box 3065 Stn 'D', Ottawa, Ontario, K1P6H6, Canada
Telephone: (613) 526 1818
Specialities: Antique architectural accessories for inside or outside the home or commercial premises; antique plumbing and lighting fixtures; Victorian spiral staircases, reproduction tin ceilings and numerous brass items.
Literature: Free on request— please specify your interest.

The Brass Knob
2311 18th Street NW, Washington, DC 20009
Telephone: (202) 332 3370
Specialities: All types of architectural antiques but in particular brass hardware items, period lighting fixtures and mantels; firebacks, columns, doors; stained, etched and leaded glass; bathrooms and bath fixtures; corbel brackets, ironwork, marble, tiles and garden ornaments.

ByGone Era Architectural Antiques
4783A Peachtree Road, Atlanta, GA 30341
Telephone: (404) 458 3016
Specialities: 30,000 square feet of architectural antiques featuring the unusual and the hard to find. Specializing in saloon decor, fine hotel furnishings, chandeliers, stained and bevelled glass, carousel art, gaming tables. Inventory arriving weekly from the US and Europe.
Special Services: Company will crate and ship. Call or write your needs. Call for personal buying service.

Canal Co
1612 14th St NW, Washington, DC 20009
Telephone: (202) 234 6637
Specialities: The Canal Company offer a wide range of architectural antiques including fully restored lighting fixtures from the 1860s through the 1930s. Their stock also features fireplace mantels, stained and leaded glass, interior and exterior doors, medicine cabinets, handrails, newel posts, and balusters, columns, brass door hardware plus pedestal sinks, iron fencing and window guards.

Gargoyles Ltd
512 South Third Street, Philadelphia, PA 19147
Telephone: (215) 629 1700
Specialities: Architectural antiques and reproductions, ironwork, fretwork, tin ceilings, bars and bar backs, leaded glass, mantels, Victorian wall units, complete store interiors, chandeliers, brackets and anything they can find. Restaurant decor, advertising memorabilia, original posters and electrical accessories. Your best bet will be a visit to their warehouse/showroom, but please call to make an appointment if out of town.
Special Services: Weekend hours by appointment.

Whit Hanks at Treaty Oak
1009 West 6th Street, Austin, TX 78703
Telephone: (512) 478 2101
Specialities: Architectural antiques, doors, entryways, fireplaces, bevelled, etched and stained glass, ironwork, panelling and panelled rooms, flooring and garden furnishings. European architectural items.

∘ GROTTO GATE ∘

Joe Ley Antiques Inc
615 East Market Street, Louisville, KY 40202
Telephone: (502) 583 4014
Specialities: A vast supplier of architectural antique items with six buildings housing over an estimated two acres of antiques. They specialize in items often hard to find including mantels, columns, newels. Other specialities include light fixtures, restaurant fittings, doors, garden ornaments, brass hardware, and a selection of iron fences and gates.

Nostalgia
307 Stiles Avenue, Savannah, GA 31401
Telephone: (912) 232 2324
Specialities: Architectural antiques of all kinds. Selection of reproduction includes dolphin downspouts, brass hardware, summer fireplace covers and balcony brackets, decorative plasterwork. Design of elegant entranceways utilising doors from England and reproduction hardware of classic designs. Bevelled and stained glass, antique and new for residential or commercial applications.
Literature: Brochures available— Simply Elegant $1.50 and Antique Stained and Beveled Glass Nostalgia $2.50

Pasternak's Emporium
2515 Morse Street, Houston, TX 77019
Telephone: (713) 528 3808
Specialities: Walk in store carries large stock of Victorian and turn-of-century architectural embellishments, such as mantels, doors, stained glass windows, brass lighting fixtures, reconditioned plumbing fixtures. Corbels, fretwork, trim and brackets in pine. Reconditioned nineteenth-century door hardware in brass bronze, also large inventory of glass doorknobs and a large selection of reconditioned brass oscillating desk fans.
Literature: Illustrated 'gingerbread' brochure $1
Special Services: Victorian gingerbread by mail order and can be custom ordered.

Rapp Restoration Supplies & Services
PO Box 308, West Suffield, CT 06093
Telephone: (203) 668 0374
Specialities: Antique building materials including chestnut and wide pine flooring, chestnut beams, planks and timbers, hand hewn beams, post and beam barn and house frames for re-assembly, weathered barn siding in silver, gold, brown and colours, roofing slate, hardware, doors and farm implements. These materials also used in restoration and true reproduction to own specifications. Hand planed wide-pine boards, board and baton doors made to order, feather edge and beaded panelling made to order.
Special Services: Design and drafting services available.

Rejuvenation House Parts Co
901 N Skidmore, Portland, Oregon, OR 97217
Telephone: (503) 249 0774
Specialities: Manufacturers of solid brass Victorian and turn-of-the-century light fixtures. All are authentic and meticulous recreations of the originals. 10,000 sq ft retail store offers antique plumbing and lighting fixtures, doors, millwork,

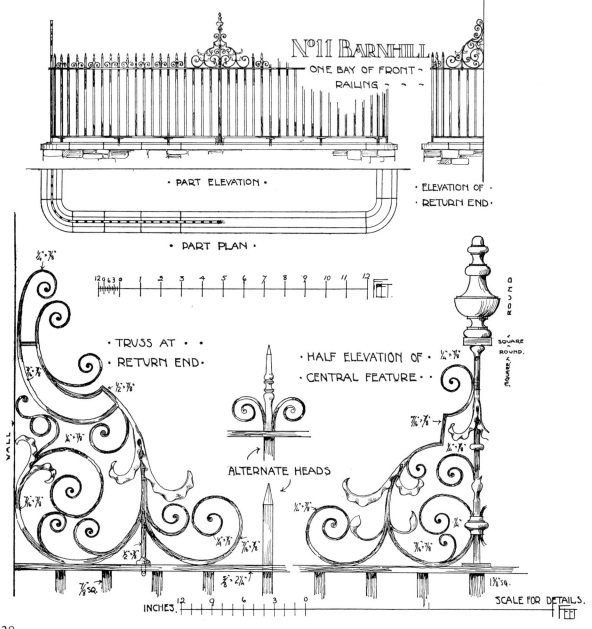

No 11 BARNHILL

ONE BAY OF FRONT RAILING

· PART ELEVATION ·

· ELEVATION OF · RETURN END ·

· PART PLAN ·

· TRUSS AT · RETURN END ·

· HALF ELEVATION OF · CENTRAL FEATURE · ·

ALTERNATE HEADS

ROUND

SQUARE · ROUND.

SQUARE.

WALL

SCALE FOR DETAILS.

INCHES.

Elevation

wrought iron. Can supply complete room interiors for restorations, or period decor in restaurants. In-stock items available for prop rentals.

Literature: Free literature available.

Greg Spiess
228–230 East Washington, Joliet, IL 60433
Telephone: (815) 722 5639
Specialities: Antique architecture ornamentation. Interior and exterior ornamental wood, mantels a speciality. Stained, leaded and bevelled glass. Antique and custom fabrication. Also handle antique tavern back bars. Antique store fixtures. Good general architectural selection.
Special Services: Custom bevelling.

Sunset Antiques/Williams Art Glass Studio
22 N Washington, Oxford, MI 48051
Telephone: (313) 628 1111
Specialities: Antique stained and bevelled glass windows, doors, sidelights. Architectural salvage including mantels, and French doors.
Special Services: Custom designing of stained, bevelled or etched glass.

United House Wrecking Corp
535 Hope Street, Stamford, CT 06907
Telephone: (203) 348 5371
Specialities: Six acres of relics from old houses, mantels, stained glass, antiques, used furniture, antique reproductions of copper weathervanes, fabulous brass and copper reproductions.
Literature: Free illustrated brochure available about the yard.

Vintage Plumbing & Sanitary Specialities
17800 Minnehaha Street, Granada Hills, CA 91344
Telephone: (818) 368 1040
Specialities: Circa 1900 American

hardware. Manufactures Craftsman 'Mission' style fixtures.
Literature: Free Craftsman Collection brochure. Mail order Catalogue available $3 includes light fixtures, cast iron roof crests.

Remodelers and Renovators
1920 North Liberty, Boise, ID 83704

Telephone: (208) 344 8612
Specialities: Suppliers of quality building, finishing and decorating products. Old style faucets, fittings, pedestal sinks in ceramic or wood, brass sinks, Victorian mouldings, fretwork and millwork. Reproduction Victorian cast aluminium spiral staircases. Reproduction hardware, screen doors, wood mouldings.

Literature: Catalogue $2.

Salvage One—The Chicago Architectural Salvage Co
1524 South Sangamon, Chicago, IL 60608
Telephone: (312) 733 0098
Specialities: Large selection of architectural artifacts including mantels, terracotta, old brass hardware, pedestal sinks, bathtubs, doors, stained glass,

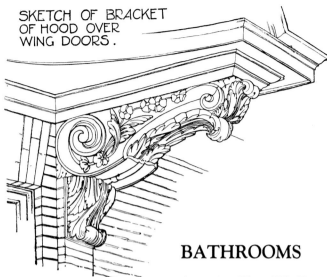

SKETCH OF BRACKET OF HOOD OVER WING DOORS.

ornamental toilets, tubs, showers, sinks in excellent original and restored condition.

Wrecking Bar of Atlanta
292 Moreland Avenue, NE, Atlanta, GA 30307
Telephone: (404) 525 0468
Specialities: One of the nation's largest collections (18,000 sq ft, three million dollar inventory) of authentic mantels, statuary, columns, capitals, wrought iron, bevelled and stained glass, and lighting fixtures. Restoration design, and installation services available.
Literature: Free literature.
Special Services: Customers providing details of decorating/restoration projects will be sent photos of in-stock items for approval.

You Name It, Inc
65 Main Street, Box 1013, Middletown, OH 45044
Telephone: (513) 932 1383
Specialities: Brokerage/consignment sales of antique, salvage and recycled building materials, houseparts, fixtures and hardware, furniture and accessories, period clothing, prints and original art, tools.
Special Services: Search service—write or call with specific requests.

BATHROOMS

Amercian Olean Tile Company
PO Box 271, Lansdale, PA 19446
Telephone: (215) 855 1111
Specialities: This major tile manufacturer makes one inch square white ceramic mosaic floor tiles and Bright White and Glass Black glazed wall tiles used in early twentieth-century bathrooms. A terracotta quarry tile is available for rustic kitchens. One inch hexagon ceramic mosaics used for foyers, baths and pantries for available in fifty-two colours. Good design flexibility for border designs.
Literature: Ceramic Mosaics Sheet 1846—free, Quarry tile sheet #1860—free, quarry tile naturals sheet #1644—free. Hexagon tile sheet #545—free

D.E.A./Bathroom Machineries
495 Main Street, Murphys, CA 95247
Telephone: (209) 728 3860
Specialities: Brass, porcelain and oak antique and reproduction bathroom fixtures.
Literature: Catalogue $2.

Restore-A-Bath and Brass
4121 Shelbyville Road, Suite G, Louisville, KY 40207
Telephone: (502) 895 2912
Specialities: Specialists in early 1900 bathrooms, restoring bathtubs including antique clawfoot tubs, pedestal sinks. They carry solid brass and

chrome plumbing fixtures for all types of sinks and tubs. Pull chain toilets also available.
Literature: Free information available.

Tennessee Tub Inc
6682 Charlotte Park, Nashville, TN 37209
Telephone: (615) 356 6515
Specialities: Antique claw footed tubs and pedestal wash basins dating from 1880s, sold completely restored. Reproduction pull chain toilets and Victorian china basins are also available. Wide selection of quality reproduction faucets and accessories.
Literature: Free brochure. Catalogue package $5.50.

Watercolors Inc
Garrison on Hudson, New York, NY 10524
Telephone: (914) 424 3327
Specialities: Exclusive importers of authentic English Edwardian and Italian traditional-style kitchen and bathroom faucet and fitting designs. All products accommodate US specifications. Washbasin sets, bathtub/shower sets, bidet and kitchen sets available in chrome, brass, gold and colorful enamel and epoxy finishes.
Literature: Full catalogue available

GARDENS

Alfresco Fine Furniture Since 1976
PO Box 1336, Durango, CO 81302
Telephone: (303) 247 9739 and 259 5743
Specialities: Redwood porch swings with deeply contoured seat and sloping back. No nails or staples. Built to last for generations. Hand finished with three coats of penetrating oil.
Literature: Colour leaflet available

Betsy's Place
323 Arch Street, Philadelphia, PA 19106
Telephone: (215) 922 3536

Specialities: A large selection of sundials and a new style sundial stand. They also have brass reproductions, tin chandeliers, pewter miniatures and historical reproductions.
Literature: Free literature

Park Place
2251 Wisconsin Avenue, NW, Washington, DC 20007
Telephone: (202) 342 6294
Specialities: Victorian garden benches and streetlamps for outdoor use. Victorian reproduction garden urns, hitching posts, mailboxes. Classic teak garden benches, tables and chairs.
Literature: Send $2 for information tailored to your individual specific requests.

Tennessee Fabricating Co
1822 Latham Street, Memphis, TN 38106
Telephone: (901) 948 3354
Specialities: Supplier of full line of aluminium and iron ornamental castings. Reproductions of lawn furniture, fountains, and urns.
Literature: Ornamental accessories booklet $2.50—Architectural ornamental metal-work $5.
Special Services: Will reproduce customers own designs or create new.

GLASS

Art Glass Studio Inc & Ernest Porcelli
333 Flatbush Avenue, Brooklyn, NY 11217
Telephone: (718) 857 6888
Specialities: Original creations in stained and leaded glass. Will also do custom work and stained and leaded glass restorations. Etched, carved and sandblasting designs.
Special Services: Free estimates with SASE.

Patrick J Curran
30 No Maple Street, Florence, MA 01060
Telephone: (413) 584 5761

130

½ PLAN AT B   ½ PLAN AT C
PLANS LOOKING VP.

DOORWAY
FROM A HOUSE
IN CAREY ST. W.C.

TOP COVERING
MISSING

PROBABLE
FACE OF
WALL

TOP CVRVED
WITH HOOD

CARVING
OMITTED

JOINT

GROVND   STEP

Specialities: Custom stained, bevelled and etched glass. Also four styles and sizes of opalescent glass table lamps. Some stained and painted glass restoration as well as bent glass repairs. Laminated, cut, polished architectural sculpture.

Literature: Slide portfolio available.

Glass Arts
30 Penniman Road, Allston, MA 02134
Telephone: (617) 661 5776

Specialities: Professional glass studio specializing in stained, bevelled and etched glass windows and lamps as well as designing and creating glass work in stained, leaded and etched glass—Victorian and other styles. Restoration of leaded windows and lamps.

Literature: Call for information or send SASE for brochure.

Special Services: Glass bending for antique lamps.

Golden Age Glassworks
339 Bellvale Road, Warwick, NY 10990
Telephone: (914) 986 1487

Specialities: Design and manufacture leaded and stained glass windows, lampshades, architectural pieces, skylights, and room dividers. Also museum quality Victorian (and other styles) reproduction and restorations. Extensive church and residential experience—in business over 12 years.

Literature: Free information, slides showing examples of work $2 per set.

Special Services: Will work from your design or help you to create one.

The Greenland Studio Inc
147 W 22nd Street, New York, NY 10011
Telephone: (212) 255 2551

Specialities: Stained glass repaired and manufactured. Expert craftsmanship for new work and restoration of all kinds of leaded glass. Tiffany windows and lampshades, painted, etched, bevelled, carved, sandblasted. Wood windows, doors and architectural trim restored or fabricated new to match historic profiles. State-of-the-art restoration techniques performed by craftsmen sensitive to the details that matter. Numerous restorations of landmarked buildings already completed. Museum quality restoration practices.

Special Services: conservator for several museum collections, including Metropolitan Museum of Art, the Cloisters, Church of St Ann and the Holy Trinity, Brooklyn, NY.

Lyn Hovey Studio Inc

266 Concord Avenue, Cambridge, MA 02138

Telephone: (617) 492 6566

Specialities: Stained and leaded glass lighting, windows, walls of glass, doors and mirrors. Distinctive original designs in Early American, Victorian and early 20th Century styles. Illuminated mirrors.

Literature: Brochures $2.

Special Services: The studio features expertise in ancient painting techniques as well as custom sashes, metal support bar systems, protective glazing and restoration.

The Kardell Studio, Inc

904 Westminster Street, NW, Washington, DC 20001

Telephone: (202) 462 4433

Specialities: A small studio specializing in leaded art glass, contemporary, Victorian, Art Deco, and Art Nouveau. Extensive knowledge of nineteenth-century ornamentation enables The Kardell Studio to design and fabricate historically appropriate art glass for all types of commercial establishments, residences and churches. (Formerly Victorian Glassworks).

Literature: Brochure and photographs $3.50

132

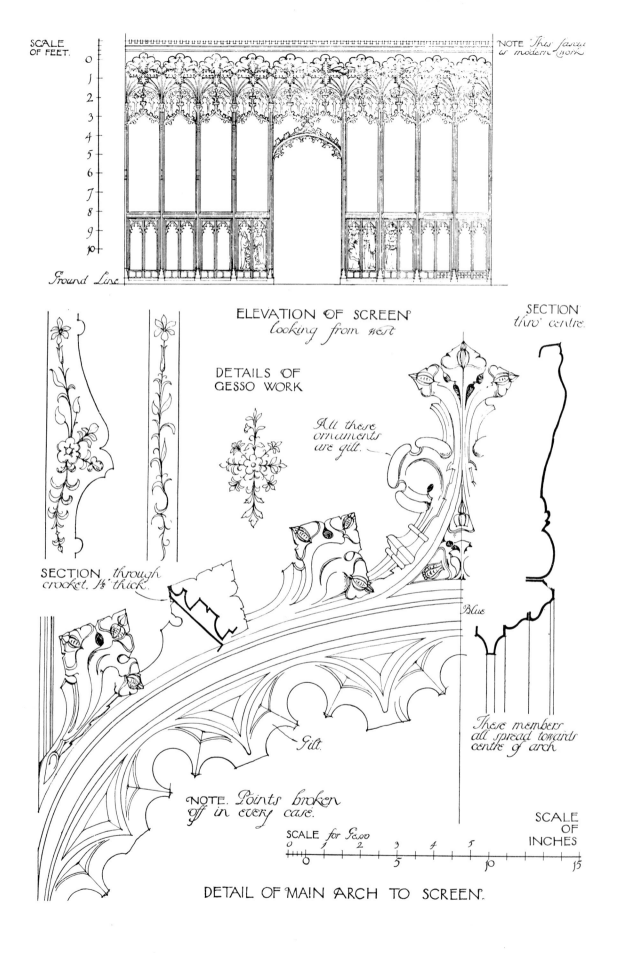

SCALE OF FEET.

NOTE *This façade is modern work*

Ground Line

ELEVATION OF SCREEN
looking from west

SECTION *thro' centre.*

DETAILS OF GESSO WORK

All these ornaments are gilt.

SECTION *through crocket. 1⅛" thick.*

Blue

These members all spread towards centre of arch

Gilt.

NOTE. *Points broken off in every case.*

SCALE *for Gesso*
0   1   2   3   4   5

SCALE OF INCHES
0   5   10   15

DETAIL OF MAIN ARCH TO SCREEN.

Special Services: Gold leaf signwork

Manor Art Glass Studio
20 Ridge Road, Douglaston,
NY 11363
Telephone: (212) 631 8029
Specialities: Carved and etched architectural glass. Professional craftsmen will restore your antique stained glass windows to their original strength and beauty.
Literature: Pictures available on specific request.
Special Services: Rosalind Brenner has designed windows for homes, fine restaurants and religious institutions throughout the country and will create new windows to blend with the period architecture of your home.

Melotte-Morse Stained Glass Inc
213 South 6th Street, Springfield,
IL 62701
Telephone: (217) 789 9515
Specialities: Melotte Morse Studio designs, fabricates and renovates stained glass art for ecclesiastical, commercial and individual clients. The studio also works extensively with existing antique glass works, performing corrective maintenance and restorative repairs or renovations. The studio has refurbished entire stained glass collections for churches and historic landmarks as well as individual panels for residential reinstallation.
Literature: Newsletter is free
Special Services: Recent renovation work includes the complete re-buildings of the State of Illinois Capitol Dome and Frank Lloyd Wright's Dana-Thomas House.

Meredith Stained Glass Studio, Inc
5700-F Sunnyside Avenue,
Beltsville, MD 20705
Telephone: (301) 345 0433 (Outside MD dial 800–448–7853 for orders only)
Specialities: Complete source for

all glass, materials and tools to build stained glass windows, lamps and decorative objects. Wholesale to trade/retail. Do it Yourself books, patterns, framing and sandblasting supplies for etched glass.
Literature: Wholesale supply catalogue available.

Newe Daisterre Glas/KaleidoArt
13431 Cedar Road, Cleveland Heights, OH 44118
Telephone: (216) 371 7500
Specialities: Custom art glass studio who works in stained and bevelled glass for commercial and residential markets. Will do etching, sandblasting, slumped glass and painting on glass. Custom framing and woodworkings such as light boxes, art glass cabinets, room dividers and partitions. Kaleidoscopes.
Literature: Free illustrated brochure.
Special Services: Will do on-location restoration of lead windows, restoration of stained and bevelled glass in studio.

Nottingham Gallery
339 Bellvale Road, Warwick,
NY 10990
Telephone: (914) 986 1487
Specialities: Imported English stained glass, both windows and doors. The glass is affordable with light, airy, elegant designs—mostly clear textures with a wonderful play of line and effectively used colours.
Literature: Write or call for free information

Pike Stained Glass Studios Inc
180 St Paul Street, Rochester,
NY 14604
Telephone: (716) 546 7570
Specialities: Design, fabrication, installation and repair of windows for churches, business and homes. Original and reproduction designs—stained, leaded, bevelled, etched glass and glass mosaics.
Literature: Free brochure, call or write for estimates.

Pocahontas Hardware and Glass
Box 127, Pocahontas, Illinois,
IL 62275
Telephone: (618) 669 2880
Specialities: Etched glass especially suited for windows, doors, transoms and cabinets. Patterns are exact reproductions of old glass.
Literature: Illustrated brochure $2.

J Ring Glass Studio Inc
2724 University Avenue SE,
Minneapolis, MN55414
Telephone: (612) 379 0920
Specialities: Fine art glass studio specializing in restoration/reproduction for major commissions. Hand bevelling, etching and engraving, stained glass work, glass painting and bending. Machine bevelling and mirror re-silvering. Reproduction of quality antique pieces.
Special Services: All custom work.

Shadovitz Bros. Distributors Inc
1565 Bergen Street, Brooklyn,
NY 11213
Telephone: (718) 774 9100
Specialities: Period picture frame mouldings and supplies, bent glass, mirrors, insulated sheets, and storm windows. Glazing tools.
Literature: Specialized catalogue available—stained, etched and bevelled decorative glass $1.

Sunburst Stained Glass Co
20 W Jennings Street, Newburgh,
IN 47630
Telephone: (812) 853 0460
Specialities: Design, construction, restoration and repair of stained, etched, and bevelled glass windows.
Literature: Brochure $3
Special Services: Services range from complete releading to minor repair to creating a new old window.

LIGHTING

Authentic Designs Inc
155 The Mill Road, West Rupert,
Vermont, VT 05776–0011
Telephone: (802) 394 7713
Specialities: Handcrafted reproductions of colonial lanterns and lighting fixtures for indoor use. Also colonial tinware, liners, pans, flower trays, boxes, kitchen hoods, and a variety of custom made items of brass, copper, galavanized, or tin.
Special Services: Send photo, sketch or line drawing of the piece you are interested in and they will build it for you.

B & P Lamp Supply Inc
Route 3, McMinnville, TN 37110
Telephone: (615) 473 3016; (800) 722 3450 (Nat); (800) 822 5267 (TN)
Specialities: Manufactures and wholesalers of reproduction lighting fixtures and parts. Selection includes hand-blown and hand-decorated glass shades, solid brass parts, and UL approved wiring components.
Literature: Complete colour catalogue and price list for dealers only $5, refundable.
Special Services: Specialize in reproductions of and parts for Gone with the Wind, Handel, Tiffany, Aladdin and Emeraldine fixtures.

A J P Coppersmith & Co
20 Industrial Parkway, Woburn,
MA 01801
Telephone: (617) 932 3700
Specialities: Authentic Colonial lighting fixtures. Chandeliers, sconces, post or wall lanterns are hand-crafted with a choice of finishes. Copper (antique or verdigris), brass, pewter type. A distinctive collection by three generations of craftsmen.
Literature: $2 for catalogue.
Special Services: Brass hardware and bath accessories also available.

Heritage Lanterns
70A Main Street, Yarmouth,

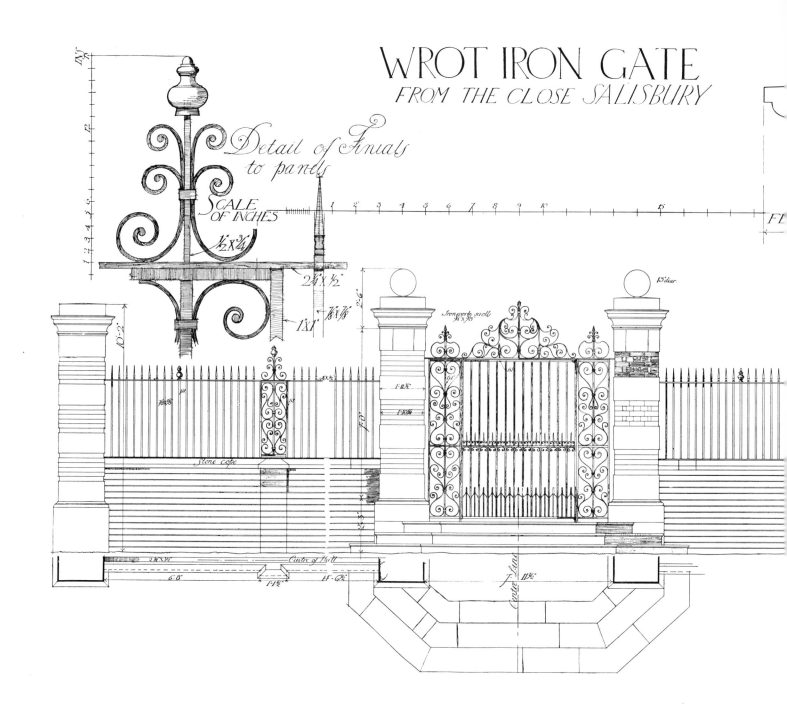

WROT IRON GATE
FROM THE CLOSE SALISBURY

Detail of Finials to panels

SCALE OF INCHES

ME 04096
Telephone: (914) 424 3327
Specialities: Wide selection of handcrafted reproduction lanterns, sconces and chandeliers for interior and exterior use. Available in brass copper or pewter.
Literature: 40 page Catalogue $3.

Light Ideas

1037 Taft Street, Rockville, MD 20850
Telephone: (301) 424 LITE
Specialities: This lamp and lighting fixture store makes reproduction Victorian, Art Deco and Nouveau style lampshades. They will also remake old lampshades. Lighting fixture glass and wire is available. Miscellaneous parts for old lamps and chandeliers.

Literature: Free estimates and brochure.
Special Services: 'We will refinish, re-wire, re-store and repair.'

METALWORK

Acquisitition and Restoration Corp
423 Massachusetts Avenue,

Indianapolis, IN 46204
Telephone: (317) 637 1266
Specialities: Reproductions of English cast-iron fireplace surrounds produced in plaster.

Agape Antiques
Box 275, Saxtons River, VT 05154
Telephone: (802) 869 2273
Specialities: Period parlour stoves

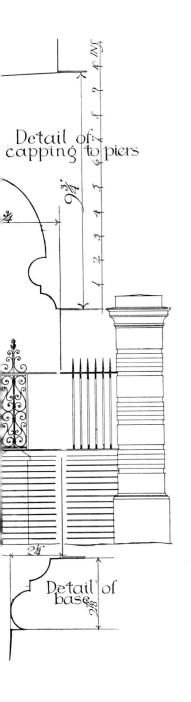

Detail of capping to piers

Detail of base

for sale, restored to original condition and ready for use. Excellent selection of stoves dating from 1800s to 1920s.
Special Services: When writing or calling for information please be specific about what you are looking for.

Anglo American Brass Co
PO Drawer 9487, San Jose,
CA 95157
Telephone: (408) 246 0203
Specialities: Authentic sand cast, die cast and stamped solid brass reproduction hardware for the restoration of furniture, doors, and cupboards. As they are manufacturers they can custom produce articles for builders, wholesalers or manufactuers. Victorian house hardware and general locks for doors, and windows. Furniture hardware.
Literature: Colour catalogue No 131 $1.50.
Special Services: Custom items produced.

Baldwin Hardware Corporation
841 E Wyomissing Blvd, Reading,
PA 19612
Telephone: (215) 777 7811
Specialities: Solid brass and interior latches, knobsets and turn pieces for period houses. Lighting fixtures, candlesticks, and accessories adapted from Early American designs.
Literature: Send $75 for colour brochure illustrating solid brass cabinet hardware, hinges, name plates, door knockers, house numbers, switch plates and other fine quality hardware items for the home.

Ball and Ball
463 W Lincoln Hwy, Exton,
PA 19341
Telephone: (215) 363 7330
Specialities: Vast selection of reproduction hardware for eighteenth- and nineteenth-century houses. In addition to all types of hardware for doors, windows and shutters.
Literature: Call or write for free mini catalogue or send $5 for complete 108 page Catalogue— revised 1983 (over 100 Victorian items now included).
Special Services: The company also supplies fixtures and will also repair locks and repair or reproduce any item of metal hardware.

Berridge Manufacturing Co
1720 Maury Street, Houston,
Texas, TX 77026
Telephone: (713) 223 4971
Specialities: Manufacturers metal roofing products, including Victorian classic and fish-scale metal shingles. Standing seam and batten seam metal roof systems are offered. These products are available in pre-finished galvanized steel, Galvalume and copper.
Literature: Free catalogue.

Blake Industries
PO Box 155, Abington, MA 02151, Express Mail Address: Blake Industries, 390 Pond Street, S. Weymark, MA 02190
Telephone: (617) 337 8772
Specialities: Promenade benches in many styles, and planters, trash receptacles, gazebos and custom built small buildings. Ornamental cast iron street light poles and fixtures. Benches in cast iron and steel and wood. Brownstone reproduction. Historic post clocks. Ornamental light poles. Cast aluminium, cast iron and wood light fixtures, cast aluminium and copper, wire mesh benches, tree guards and trash.
Literature: Please specify your interest for a free brochure.
Special Services: Custom build service.

Bona Decorative Hardware
3073 Madison Road, Cincinnati,
OH 45209
Telephone: (513) 321 7877
Specialities: Decorative hardware—mostly formal French and English in style. Bathroom fittings and accessories—several designs are appropriate for period houses. Also black iron door and cabinet hardware, brass rim locks, porcelain door knobs, fireplace tools and accessories. Also of interest are their brass bar rail hardware and brass sliding door pulls, faucets for footed tubs and brass sinks.
Literature: Illustrated catalogue and price list $2

The Brass Finial
Dept. A, 2408 Riverton Road,
Cinnaminson, NJ 08077
Telephone: (609) 786 9337
Specialities: Offers fine quality brass products including hard-to-find door and cabinet hinges, door lever sets, and replicas of Victorian plumbing fixtures. Also has a selection of interior accessories in coordinating styles to finish any restoration project. Generous quantity discounts and a variety of metal finishes along with a complete guarantee of satisfaction.
Literature: Catalogue $1

Brass Menagerie
524 St Louis Street, New Orleans,
LA 70130
Telephone: (504) 524 0921
Specialities: Solid brass hardware and locks of all periods, antique and reproduction. Porcelain and wrought iron hardware, rim locks, unusual hardware, bra rails, solid brass drapery and curtain hardware, fireplace hooks, chandeliers, wall brackets and sconces. Bathroom fixtures and accessories of American and European design, including period toilets, with wall hung tanks, decorated sink bowls and turn of the century pedestal type sinks.
Literature: Free brochure.

Bryant Stove Works Inc
Box 2048, Rich Road, Thorndike,
Maine, ME 04986
Telephone: (207) 568 3665
Specialities: Family owned business restores and then sells antique cast iron cookstoves and parlour heaters. They specialize in old kitchen ranges. Search service finds rare stoves for museums and historic restorations. Large stock of antique parts. Player pianos, one of a kind stove part clocks.

The Bryant Stove Museum is a collection of rare stoves.
Literature: Free flyers and catalogue
Special Services: Shipping can be arranged anywhere

Circast Inc
380 7th Street, San Francisco,
CA 94103
Telephone: (415) 863 8319
Specialities: An outstanding
collection of reproduction
hardware, late 1870s to mid
1880s bronze doorknobs, hinges,
keyholes and sash lifts
reproduced from original
pattern. Other metals available.
Literature: Catalogue
Special Services: Write for nearest
dealer.

The Copper House
RFD 1 Rt 4, Epsom, NH 03234
Telephone: (603) 736 9798
Specialities: Handmade copper
weathervanes, lanterns for post,
wall or hanging. Authentic
reproductions. Variety of styles
and sizes available. Flagpole balls
and weathervane parts and
cupolas.
Literature: Catalogue $2

Crawford's Old House Store
301 McCall Street, Waukesha,
WI 53186
Telephone: (414) 542 0685 and
(800) 556 7878
Specialities: A wide variety of old
house items, including authentic
Victorian reproduction door and
window hardware, lighting and
plumbing supplies, reproduction
marble fireplace mantels, wood
corner blocks, finials, door stops,
corner beads, and reference books.
Literature: Free brochure

Duvinage Corporation
PO Box 828, Hagerstown,
MD 21741–0828
Telephone: (301) 733 8255
Specialities: Manufactures
complete lines of spiral and
circular stairway systems for
residential, commercial and
industrial application—interior
and exterior use.
Literature: Free brochure.
Special Services: Circular and
spiral stairs are custom built to
your specification.

18th Century Hardware Co.,
131 East 3rd Street, Derry,

136

DETAILS OF
IRONWORK

PA 15627
Telephone: (412) 694 2708
Specialities: Reproduction
hardware in brass, porcelain and
black iron covering Early
American and Victorian periods.
Pulls, knobs, casters, hinges,
hooks, latches, door knockers,
and other brass accessories.
Literature: Catalogue $3

Elephant Hill Ironworks
RR #1, Box 168, Tunbridge,
Vermont, VT 05077
Telephone: (802) 889 9444
Specialities: A small company
producing accurate
reproductions of seventeenth-,
eighteenth- and early

nineteenth-century hardware.
Custom work undertaken, gates,
and railings. Household
ironwork including reproduction
fireplace tools, ladles, forks,
skimmers, cranes, clock jacks,
boot scrapers, candlestands, and
pipe tongs.
Literature: Catalogue $2.
Special Services: All items are
hand forged and finished to
ensure an authentic
representation of pieces of the
period.

Elmira Stove Works
22 Church Street W, Elmira,
Ontario, Canada, N3B 1M3
Telephone: (519) 669 5103
Specialities: Wood or coal burning
cast iron cookstoves. Many are
copies of turn of the century
designs. Also produces fireplaces
inserts and classic electric
cooking ranges.
Literature: Colour brochure $1.
Special Services: Distributors
throughout Canada and United
States

The Farm Forge
6945 Fishburg Road, Dayton,
OH 45424
Telephone: (513) 233 6751
Specialities: Mr Wood offers a
complete selection of
reproduction and restoration
hardware, lighting and
architectural iron work in
traditional or contemporary
styles.
Literature: Catalogue $1.
Special Services: Hand forged and
custom items

**Debbie Fellenze, Hardware &
Antiques**
2216 Cherokee Street, St Louis,
MO 63118
Telephone: (314) 776 8363
Specialities: Antique shop
specializing in brass and copper
fixtures. Lighting, bath fixtures,
door hardware, and glass globes.

Lemee's Fireplace Equipment
815 Bedford Street, Bridgewater,
MA 02324
Telephone: (617) 697 2672

Specialities: Bellows and fireplace
accessories and equipment. All
types of iron hardware—and-
irons, firesets, and cast iron
grates.
Literature: Illustrated catalogue
and price list of fireplace
equipment $1 deductible from
first order.

Mill River Hammerworks
Ned James—Metalsmith, 65 Canal
Street, Turners Falls, MA 01376
Telephone: (413) 863 8388
Specialities: Interior and exterior
architectural hardware, gates,
railings, grilles, lanterns,
chandeliers, furnishings and
miscellany.
Literature: Brochure available
Special Services: Difficult or
unusual antique repair or
reproduction a speciality.

Moultrie Manufacturing Company
PO Drawer 1179, Moultrie,
GA 31776–1179
Telephone: (in Georgia) 1 912 985
1312 or toll-free 1–800 841 8674
Specialities: Architectural
metalwork including Old South
aluminum columns, the Old
South Collection of cast garden
furniture. Decorative gates and
fences.
Literature: Full catalogues of all
products available
Special Services: Planning and
design kits for architects and
builders available on request

Paxton Hardware Inc
Dept AA1, 7818 Bradshaw Road,
Upper Falls, Maryland, MA 21156
Telephone: (301) 592 8505
Specialities: Paxton Hardware
maintain a large selection of hard
to find restoration items
including brass furniture pulls
and knobs from Queen Anne to
contemporary, furniture locks,
casters, table slides, bed
hardware, chair cane, hinges,
mirror screws and much more.
They also stock an extensive line
of reproduction lamp fittings and
glass lamp shades.
Literature: Full Catalogue $3.50 +
free mini catalogue

Schwartz's Forge and Metalworks Inc

PO Box 205, Deansboro, NY 13328
Telephone: (315) 841 4477
Specialities: Design and execution of architectural ironwork in a variety of styles, for use as gates, railings, grilles, and furnishings. Traditional blacksmithing work used on all projects.
Literature: Representative portfolio available $3.50.
Special Services: Custom design work.

Travis Tuck Inc—Metal Sculptor

Box 1832A, Martha's Vineyard, MA 02568
Telephone: (617) 693 3914
Specialities: Custom metal work studio specializing in copper weathervanes. Sculptured copper tables and fountains are also available to client's specifications.
Literature: Brochures $1
Special Services: Custom copper work

PLASTERWORK & DECORATION

Architectural Sculpture

242 Lafayette Street, New York, NY 10012
Telephone: (212) 431 5873
Specialities: Custom order and in-stock cast plaster ornament—medallions, mouldings, brackets, capitals, plaques, and sculptures. Specializing in Neo classic and turn-of-the-century restoration ornament. Showroom Tuesday to Friday, 10am to 6pm, Saturday 12 noon to 5pm
Literature: Catalogue $3.
Special Services: They have replicated pieces for many landmark NYC interiors

Casey Architectural Specialities

1615 N Warren Avenue, Milwaukee, WI 53202
Telephone: (414) 765 9531
Specialities: Ornamental plasterer does stock and custom

mouldings, restoration, residential or commercial work. They will recreate period ceilings, make cement castings for exterior ornaments and will make patterns to your specifications.

Special Services: Operates mainly in the Wisconsin area but can travel.

Chester Granite Co
Algeriie Road, Blandford, MA 01008
Telephone: (413) 269 4287
Specialities: Stone masons specializing in using traditional techniques and hand tools to produce architectural details such as door steps, pillars, quoins, window sills and lintels. Available in granite, marble or brownstone. Also available quarried blue-grey granite.
Special Services: Work is done from architectural drawings or samples.

Classic Architectural Specialities
5302 Junius, Dallas, TX 75214
Telephone: (214) 827 5111
Specialities: Restoration/ renovation products source. Doors, mouldings and turnings in stock. Custom made and stock screen doors, gingerbread, fretwork, Victorian design porch swings, park benches, lamp posts, entry doors, gargoyles, newels and mantels.
Literature: Catalogue $3.
Special Services: Design consultation available to customers.

Designer Resource
5160 Melrose Avenue, Los Angeles, CA 90038
Telephone: (213) 465 9235
Specialities: Complete selection of period and hard to find architectural detail. Stock and custom designs in columns, mantels, metal ceilings, composition ornament, architectural plaster detail, carved, embossed wood mouldings, metal mouldings, and plaster cornices.

Literature: Extensive catalogues are available, please write or call for list.
Special Services: Designer Resource sells to designers, architects and builders but will sell to the serious individual restoring a period home.

Felber Studios Inc
110 Ardmore Avenue, Ardmore, PA 19003
Telephone: (215) 642 4710
Specialities: Felber Studios Inc maintains a collection of 2,200 plus original antique ornamental castings. Ceiling medallions, cornices, cartouches and niche shells are stocked.
Literature: Catalogue available $2
Special Services: They create new or restore period plaster mouldings and ornaments.

David Flaharty—Sculptor
79 Magazine Road, R.D. 1, Green Lane, PA 18054
Telephone: (215) 234 8242
Specialites: Specialises in the reproduction and restoration of architectural details and ornaments, especially in plaster and fibre glass.
Literature: Photos of work supplied for serious enquiries.
Special Services: Among his clients are the State Department, the White House, the U.S. Capitol, Georgetown University, Metropolitan Museum of Art.

C G Girolami and Co
944 N Spaulding Avenue, Chicago, IL 60651
Telephone: (312) 227 1959
Specialities: They manufacture an extensive line of ceilings, brackets, capitals, columns, and fireplaces. Available in many styles—Old English, Spanish, Gothic and French. All reproductions are hand cast of hard plaster reinforced with hemp fiber. Exterior reproductions available in cement.
Literature: Architectural Reproduction catalogues $3,

Mantels and Fireplaces, Ornamental Plaster and Cast Stone
Special Services: This company formed in 1913 restores, reproduces and/or redesigns turn-of-the-century plaster architectural work including cornices, mouldings, rosettes, and reliefs.

Koeppel/Freedman Studios
368 Congress Street, 5th Floor, Boston, MA 02210
Telephone: (617) 426 8887
Specialities: This small company specialises in custom architectural restoration and design, including mould making, hand remodelling, and creation of new ornaments for appropriate application within the context of existing architecture. Interior work in cast iron, reinforced plaster or a combination of plaster and fibreglass. Most exterior work is cast in epoxy-fibreglass, cement or a combination of these.
Literature: Free information.
Special Services: Painting services. Colour matching, recreation of original processes and decorative painting or restored plasterwork. Painted furniture, trompe l'oeil murals and decorative finishes.

Frank J Mangione Plaster and Stucco
21 John Street, Saugerties, NY 12477
Telephone: (914) 246 9863
Specialities: Specializes in the restoration of ornamental plasterwork. Will also reproduce plaster domes and mouldings.
Special Services: Serving New York/Connecticut area.

Russell Restoration of Suffolk
Rte 1 Box 243A, Mattituck, NY 11952
Telephone: (516) 765 2481
Specialities: Quality restoration of ornamental plaster and lath plaster (flat work), cornice mouldings, ceilings, medallions and brackets. Also custom niches, columns, light domes,

and other architectural detail. Any period or style from Colonial to Art Deco. Also restoration of masonry and re-pointing in original materials.
Special Services: Custom work only

David Woods Plaster Restoration

"THE ALCOVE" KENSINGTON GARDENS.

PLAN AS AT PRESENT

KEEPERS   GARDENERS

COVE

DAWSON. MENS & DELT. 1902

129 Academy Street, Poughkeepsie, NY 12601
Telephone: (914) 471 9832
Specialities: Plain and ornamental plastering using period techniques. Run in place cornices, mouldings and recasting or original ornaments.
Special Services: Will restore or recreate period interiors, teaches plaster restoration.

WOOD AND MILLWORK

American Woodworking
2856 Aiello Drive, San Jose, CA 95111
Telephone: (408) 227 5533
Specialities: Fireplace mantels, architectural panelling for walls and ceilings, and pre-fabricated wainscotting; bars and libraries comprise much of their work (San Francisco Bay area preferred). Architectural interior millwork and cabinetry—fireplaces, bars, libraries, wainscot panelling, ceiling systems.
Literature: Brochures available $1.50

Architectural Components
PO Box 249, Leverett, MA 01054
Telephone: (413) 367 9441
Specialities: Produces and supplies eighteenth- and nineteenth-century architectural millwork. Interior and exterior doors; small pane window sashes, plank window frames and a variety of reproduction mouldings patterned after Connecticut Valley architecture.
Literature: Send $3 for brochure or call.
Special Services: Custom work; panelled fireplace walls, pediments, shutters, fan lights, French doors and period entrances.

Bare Wood Inc
106 Ferris Street, Brooklyn, New York, NY 11231
Telephone: (718) 875 9037
Specialities: Custom manufacture of eighteenth- and nineteenth-century architectural millwork, interior and exterior. Large selection of antique architectural accessories, doors, mantels, staircase parts. London-trained craftsmen include hand-carvers, turners, and cabinet makers. Bare Wood specialize in custom restoration or duplication in your choice of wood.
Literature: Free flyer.
Special Services: Consulting service available. Inquiries should be specific.

Bartley's Mill—Victorian Woodwork
8515 San Leandro Street, Oakland, CA 94621
Telephone: (415) 569 5533
Specialities: Wooden mouldings and Victorian woodwork reproduction. Custom and stock items.
Literature: 67 page catalogue with 700 moulding cross sections.

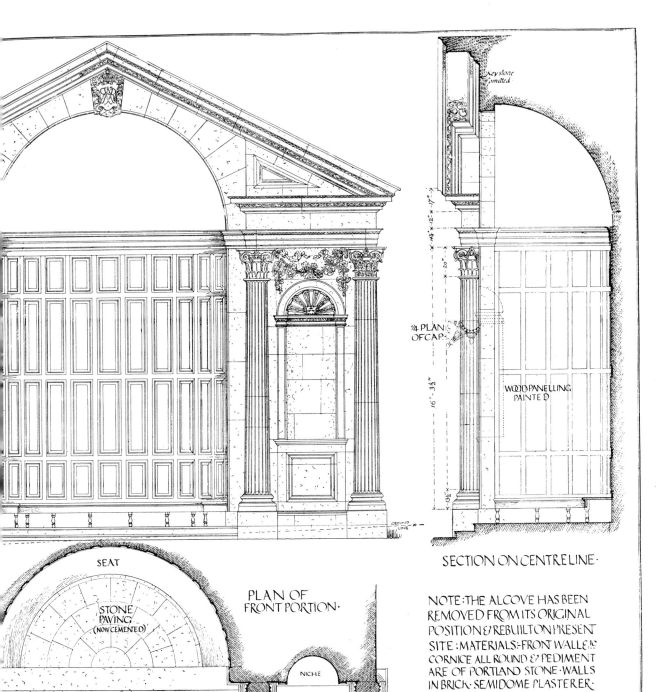

SECTION ON CENTRE LINE·

PLAN OF FRONT PORTION·

SEAT

STONE PAVING (NOW CEMENTED)

NICHE

STEP·

NOTE: THE ALCOVE HAS BEEN REMOVED FROM ITS ORIGINAL POSITION & REBUILT ON PRESENT SITE· MATERIALS: FRONT WALLS CORNICE ALL ROUND & PEDIMENT ARE OF PORTLAND STONE· WALLS IN BRICK· SEMIDOME PLASTERER·

Special Services: Sales offices located in Oakland and San Francisco

Boston Turning Works
42 Plympton Street, Boston, MA 02118
Telephone: (617) 482 9085
Specialities: Producers of custom woodturnings: balusters, newel posts, porch posts, columns, column bases and caps, rosettes and finials
Special Services: Copies and replicas can be made from sample, fragment or drawing.

Cumberland Woodcraft Co
PO Drawer 609, Carlisle, PA 17013
Telephone: (717) 243 0063
Specialities: Leading manufactuer in Victorian millwork. Architectural hand carvings, brackets, corbels, grilles, fretwork, turnings, plus special treatments. Also available raised panel ceiling treatments, bars, partitions, wainscotting. All crafted in solid oak or poplar.
Literature: 32 page full colour catalogue and price list available $3.50.
Special Services: Special treatments available.

Dimension Lumber Co
517 Stagg Street, Brooklyn, NY 11237
Telephone: (718) 497 1680
Specialities: Complete milling facilities for custom fabrication of mouldings and trim, dressed four sides in any hardwood and most softwoods. Also mills hardwood to your specifications. No minimum amounts.
Special Services: They can match original mouldings with samples, plaster casts or blue prints.

The Fireplace Mantel Shop Inc
4217 Howard Avenue, Kensington, Maryland, MD 20895
Telephone: (301) 564 1550
Specialities: Architectural woodwork, specializing in decorative wood mantels, entrance sets and cornices and

mouldings.
Literature: 22 page Wood Moulding & Millwork catalogue $3.50
Special Services: Custom millwork, panels and doors.

The Gazebo and Porchworks
728 9th Avenue SW, Puyallup, WA 98371–6744
Telephone: (206) 848 0502
Specialities: A small family business offering a selection of wood turnings, spindles, newels and porch posts. Corner brackets, corbels, gable trims, porch swings, and arbors.
Literature: Catalogue $2

International Building Components
Box 51, Glenwood, New York, NY 14069
Telephone: (716) 592 2953
Specialities: Cupolas, carved wooden mantels, replacement doors and frames, oak, cherry, mahogany and walnut wood doors, and spiral and circular stair components. Also decorative moulded millwork and cabinetry, butcher block counter tops, wood, aluminium or fiberglass columns, decorative hardware, church pews and pulpits. Sold through distributors.
Literature: Product literature free—please specify interest.

Mark Knudsen
1100 E County Line Road, Des Moines, IA 50320
Telephone: (515) 285 6112
Specialities: Wood carver and turner who offers a full range of custom woodworking services. Duplication of moulding, ornament, and gingerbread, fancy joinery, stair parts, porch posts, doors and windows, repair and reproduction of fine period furniture.
Special Services: Machine turning. Please contact for specific information.

Mad River Wood Works
PO Box 163, 1355 Giuntoli Lane,

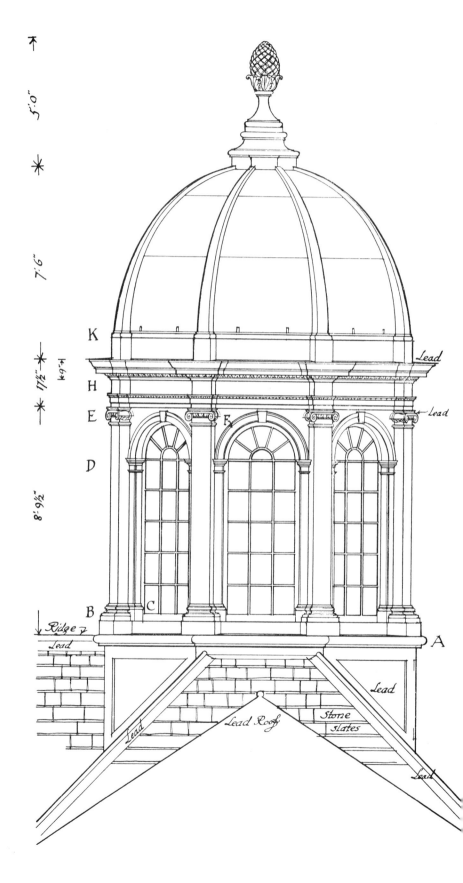

Arcata, CA 95521
Telephone: (707) 826 0629
Specialities: Manufacturers of Victorian millwork in redwood and select hardwoods. Several patterns of ornamental shingles, turnings, ornamental trim,. mouldings, old style screen door replicas, corbels, brackets, balusters and railing and ornamental pickets. Gable treatments.
Literature: Catalogue $2.50
Special Services: Custom work is also accepted.

Maple Hill Woodworking
RD2, Ballston Spa, NY 12020
Telephone: (518) 885 7258
Specialities: Mouldings and millwork made to order for restoration and reproduction of period homes and antique furniture. They specialize in exact reproduction of existing mouldings in large or small quantities. Fireplace mantels.
Special Services: Authentic reproductions of batten doors made to order.

Maurer & Shepherd, Joyners Inc
122 Naubuc Avenue, Glastonbury, CT 06033
Telephone: (203) 633 2383
Specialities: Handcrafted custom-made interior and exterior eighteenth-century architectural trim. Finely-detailed Colonial doors and windows, shutters, wainscot and wall panelling, carved details and pediments. Antique glass also available.
Literature: Free brochure.

North Pacific Joinery
76 West Fourth Street, Eureka, CA 95501
Telephone: (707) 443 5788
Specialities: Custom fabrication of redwood windows—any size or design. Custom doors—entry systems and French door systems. Newel posts, balusters, handrails, toerails and mouldings.
Literature: Catalogue $3 or call or write with specific request.
Special Services: Design service available.

Old House—New House Restorations
169 North Victoria Street, Saint Paul, MN 55104
Telephone: (612) 227 7127
Specialities: Carpentry, general contracting—specialize in restoration of Victorian houses and commercial structures, reproduction mouldings, spindle work.
Special Services: Custom millwork, mantels, stairparts and turnings.

Old World Moulding and Finishing Co Inc
115 Allen Boulevard, Farmingdale, NY 11735
Telephone: (516) 293 1789
Specialities: Hardwood embossed mouldings, cornices, baseboards, mantels and a modular system of panelling suitable for a variety of period styles.
Literature: Colour catalogue and price list $2.
Special Services: custom work also done.

W P Stephens Lumber Co
PO Box 1267, 145 Church Street, Marietta, GA 30060
Telephone: (404) 428 1531
Specialities: Architectural millwork includes mouldings, sidings, flooring, panelling, doors, shutters, mantels and cabinet work.
Literature: Stock moulding catalogue $1.
Special Services: Can match customer profiles.

Strobel Millwork
PO Box 84, Route 7, Cornwall Bridge, CT 06754
Telephone: (203) 672 6727
Specialities: Stock and custom architectural millwork. Company specializes in the exact duplication of all styles of wood windows, doors, and entrance frames, particularly Italianate or Renaissance styles.
Literature: Brochure available $2.

Vintage Wood Works
Dept. 913, 513 S. Adams,

Fredericksburg, TX 78624
Telephone: (512) 997 9513
Specialities: Produces a line of authentic Victorian gingerbread, hand crafted of solid pine for interior and exterior. Porch turnings, corbels, gable decorations, gazebos and more.
Literature: Illustrated catalogue $2
Special Services: Custom length spandrels, shelves, and window cornices.

Jack Wallis Doors
Rt 1 Box 22A, Murray, KY 42071
Telephone: (502) 489 2613
Specialities: A large selection of handcrafted doors, with stained, etched or bevelled glass insets. Complete entryways, side lights, transoms.
Literature: Colour catalogue $3
Special Services: Custom make any type of wood door and glass.

Frederick Wilbur, Carver
PO Box 425, Lovingston, VA 22949
Telephone: (804) 263 4827
Specialities: Specializes in architectural hand carving and shaping. Most work is commissioned by architects, interior decorators.
Literature: Free brochure.
Special Services: Carving for individuals is considered.

Women's Woodwork Construction
26 Adam Street, Newton, MA 02160
Telephone: (617) 964 6496
House carpentry services: Victorian and old house restorations. Interior remodelling, designs and plans. Licensed and insured.
Literature: Portfolio available.

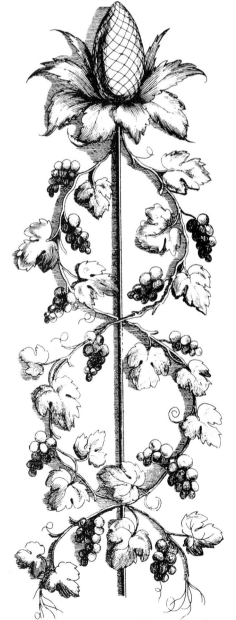

Vine leaves and Grapes dropt from a Pine for the face of a Pilaster or any place required

INDEX

Acknowledgements

Alan Robertson and Douglas Unwin would like to acknowledge the very special help the following people have given:

Mr and Mrs Robert Aagaard; Mr Peter Brown, Director of Fairfax House, York; Mr and Mrs John Buckle and Mrs Melanie Buckle, Havenplan (Architectural Antiques) Ltd, The Old Station, Killamarsh, Sheffield; Cochrane, Flynn-Roger and Williams, Architects, 122 South Circular Rd, Dublin; Dean and Chapter of York Minster; Mr and Mrs N. G. Fulton; Grierson Gower and Malcolm Gliksten, Brillscote Farm Auctions, Lea, Malmesbury; Mr Conal Gregory; Mrs H. D. Hill; Historic House Hotels at Middlethorpe Hall Hotel, Bishopthorpe Rd, York; Mr and Mrs Dennis Law, Manor Antiques, Stillington; Machin Designs Ltd, Ransome's Dock, Parkgate Rd, London for the use of the pictures on pp. 70 and 71; George and Jean Milton and Joan Deering; Mr and Mrs Adrian Palmer; Mr Gordon Reece, The Gordon Reece Gallery, Finkle St, Knaresborough; Mr James Rylands, Sothebys, Summers Place, Billingshurst; Mrs S. B. Spencer; Andy Thornton, Andy Thornton Architectural Antiques, Ainsleys Industrial Estate, Elland for the use of the pictures on pp. 92–3 and 96–7; Mr and Mrs H. A. Schmidt; Mr Robert Stavely; and St Wilfrid's Church, York, for the archive photograph shown on p. 17.

Special thanks go to the editor, Barbara Fuller, of Unwin Hyman; to Elizabeth Palmer, the designer; to David Harriman of Leeds for printing the black and white photographs; to Michael Fong of York for technical photographic assistance; and to Linda Combi for the line illustrations.